casual cooking

Have your bake & eat it

casual cooking

Have your bake & eat it

LOVE FOOD™

This edition published by Parragon Books Ltd in 2015
LOVE FOOD is an imprint of Parragon Books Ltd

Parragon Books Ltd
Chartist House
15–17 Trim Street
Bath BA1 1HA, UK
www.parragon.com/lovefood

ISBN 978-1-4723-8485-0
Printed in China

Cover photography by Charlie Richards
Designed by Beth Kalynka
Nutritional analysis by Judith Wills

Notes for the Reader
This book uses both metric and imperial measurements. Follow the same units of measurement
throughout; do not mix metric and imperial. All spoon measurements are level: teaspoons are
assumed to be 5 ml, and tablespoons are assumed to be 15 ml. Unless otherwise stated, milk is
assumed to be full fat, eggs and individual vegetables are medium, and pepper is freshly ground
black pepper. Unless otherwise stated, all root vegetables should be peeled prior to using.

Garnishes, decorations and serving suggestions are all optional and not necessarily included
in the recipe ingredients or method. Any optional ingredients and seasoning to taste are not
included in the nutritional analysis. The times given are an approximate guide only. Preparation
times differ according to the techniques used by different people and the cooking times may
also vary from those given. Optional ingredients, variations or serving suggestions have not
been included in the time calculations. Nutritional values are per serving (Serves...) or per item
(Makes...).

Bundt ® is a registered trademark of Northland Aluminum Products, Inc.

contents

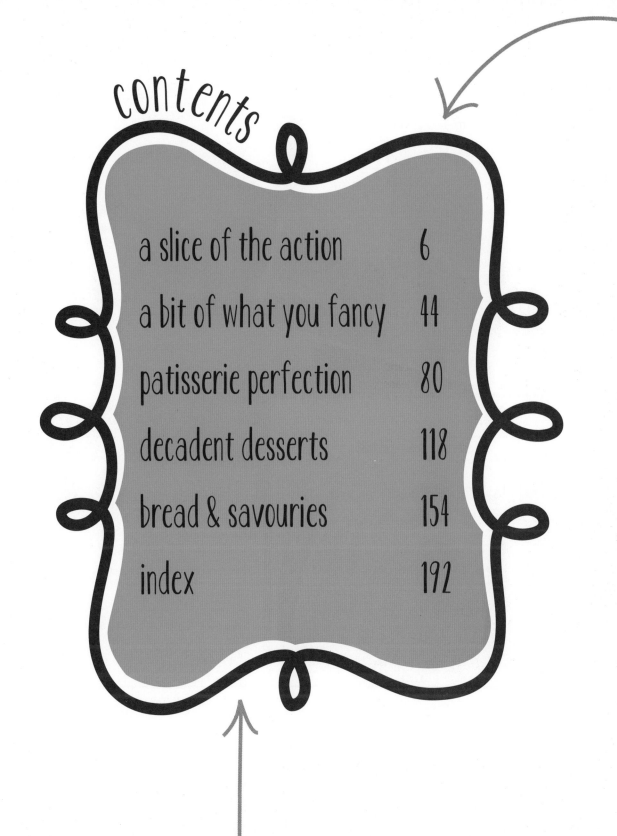

a slice of the action   6

a bit of what you fancy   44

patisserie perfection   80

decadent desserts   118

bread & savouries   154

index   192

Nothing shows you care like a home-baked cake! Whether light and fruity or rich and gooey, a large cake is ideal for sharing and makes a great centrepiece for any special occasion. It's also easier to transport than individual cakes — just add napkins and you're ready to serve!

a slice of the action

classic chocolate cake	8
lemon drizzle cake	10
victoria sponge cake	12
rich fruit cake	14
frosted carrot cake	16
coffee bundt cake	18
dorset apple cake	20
sticky toffee pudding	22
coconut layer cake	24
LINING CAKE TINS	26
red velvet cake	28
hot chocolate fudge layer cake	30
polenta & blueberry loaf cake	32
pumpkin spice cake	34
raspberry & almond cake	36
soured cream cake with nectarines	38
cookie ice-cream cake	40
piñata party cake	42

classic chocolate cake

prep: 35 mins, plus cooling and chilling
cook: 30-35 mins

55 g/2 oz cocoa powder

7 tbsp boiling water

200 g/7 oz unsalted butter, softened,
  plus extra for greasing

125 g/4½ oz caster sugar

70 g/2½ oz soft light brown sugar

4 eggs, beaten

1 tsp vanilla extract

200 g/7 oz self-raising flour

frosting

200 g/7 oz plain chocolate,
  broken into pieces

115 g/4 oz unsalted butter

100 ml/3½ fl oz double cream

top tip

If you're pushed for time, simply use a tub of shop-bought chocolate fudge frosting to fill and top this cake.

1. Preheat the oven to 180°C/350°F/
Gas Mark 4. Grease two 20-cm/8-inch
sandwich tins and line with baking paper.

2. Blend the cocoa powder and water to a
smooth paste and set aside. Put the butter,
caster sugar and brown sugar into a large
bowl and beat together until pale and
creamy. Gradually beat in the eggs, then
stir in the cocoa paste and vanilla extract.
Sift in the flour and fold in gently.

3. Divide the mixture between the prepared
tins. Bake in the preheated oven for
25–30 minutes, or until risen and just springy
to the touch. Leave to cool in the tins for
5 minutes, then turn out onto a wire rack to
cool completely.

4. To make the frosting, put the chocolate
and butter into a heatproof bowl set over
a saucepan of gently simmering water and
heat until melted. Remove from the heat
and stir in the cream. Leave to cool for
20 minutes, then chill in the refrigerator for
40–50 minutes, stirring occasionally, until
thick enough to spread.

5. Sandwich the sponges together with half
the frosting, then spread the remainder over
the top of the cake.

cals: 585   fat: 41.1g   sat fat: 25.2g   fibre: 4g   carbs: 48.4g   sugar: 27.3g   salt: 0.7g   protein: 7.5g

lemon drizzle cake

prep: 25–30 mins, plus cooling
cook: 50–55 mins

2 eggs

175 g/6 oz caster sugar

150 g/5½ oz soft margarine,
  plus extra for greasing

finely grated rind of 1 lemon

175 g/6 oz self-raising flour

125 ml/4 fl oz milk

icing sugar, for dusting

syrup

140 g/5 oz icing sugar

50 ml/2 fl oz lemon juice

top tip

It is important to leave the cake in the tin until it is completely cool so that the cake absorbs the delicious lemon syrup.

1. Preheat the oven to 180°C/350°F/Gas Mark 4. Grease an 18-cm/7-inch square cake tin and line with baking paper.

2. Place the eggs, caster sugar and margarine in a mixing bowl and beat hard until smooth and fluffy. Stir in the lemon rind, then fold in the flour lightly and evenly. Stir in the milk, mixing evenly, then spoon into the prepared tin, smoothing level.

3. Bake in the preheated oven for 45–50 minutes, or until golden brown and firm to the touch. Remove from the oven and stand the tin on a wire rack.

4. To make the syrup, place the icing sugar and lemon juice in a small saucepan and heat gently, stirring until the sugar dissolves. Do not boil.

5. Prick the warm cake all over with a skewer, and spoon the hot syrup evenly over the top, allowing it to be absorbed.

6. Leave to cool completely in the tin, then turn out the cake, cut into 12 pieces and dust with a little icing sugar before serving.

cals: 260   fat: 10.7g   sat fat: 2.9g   fibre: 0.4g   carbs: 38.9g   sugar: 27.8g   salt: 0.7g   protein: 3g

victoria sponge cake

prep: 25 mins, plus cooling
cook: 25-30 mins

175 g/6 oz self-raising flour

1 tsp baking powder

175 g/6 oz unsalted butter, softened,
  plus extra for greasing

175 g/6 oz golden caster sugar

3 eggs

icing sugar, for dusting

filling

3 tbsp raspberry jam

300 ml/10 fl oz double cream, whipped

16 fresh strawberries, hulled and
  halved

1. Preheat the oven to 180°C/350°F/Gas
Mark 4. Grease two 20-cm/8-inch sandwich
tins and line with baking paper.

2. Sift the flour and baking powder into a bowl
and add the butter, caster sugar and eggs. Mix
together, then beat well until smooth.

3. Divide the mixture between the prepared
tins and smooth the surfaces. Bake in the
preheated oven for 25–30 minutes, or until
well risen, golden brown and just springy
to the touch. Leave to cool in the tins for
5 minutes, then turn out onto a wire rack
to cool completely.

4. Sandwich the cakes together with the
raspberry jam, whipped double cream and
strawberry halves. Dust with icing sugar.

top tip

To create a lacy pattern on top of the
cooked cake, place a doily over the cake
before dusting with icing sugar.

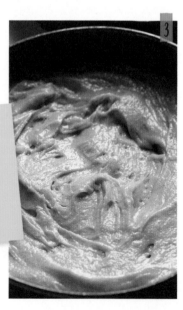

cals: 550   fat: 38.8g   sat fat: 23.7g   fibre: 1.2g   carbs: 45.3g   sugar: 27.6g   salt: 0.9g   protein: 5.7g

rich fruit cake

prep: 30-35 mins, plus soaking and cooling
cook: 2¼-2¾ hours

350 g/12 oz sultanas

225 g/8 oz raisins

115 g/4 oz ready-to-eat
dried apricots, chopped

85 g/3 oz stoned dates, chopped

4 tbsp dark rum or brandy (optional)

juice and finely grated rind of 1 orange

225 g/8 oz unsalted butter, softened,
plus extra for greasing

225 g/8 oz light muscovado sugar

4 eggs, beaten

70 g/2½ oz chopped mixed peel

85 g/3 oz glacé cherries, quartered

25 g/1 oz chopped glacé
ginger or stem ginger

40 g/1½ oz blanched almonds,
chopped

200 g/7 oz plain flour

1 tsp ground mixed spice

1. Place the sultanas, raisins, apricots and dates in a large bowl and stir in the rum, if using, orange juice and rind. Cover and leave to soak for several hours or overnight.

2. Preheat the oven to 150°C/300°F/Gas Mark 2. Grease a 20-cm/8-inch round cake tin and line with baking paper.

3. Beat the butter and sugar together until pale and creamy. Gradually beat in the eggs, beating hard after each addition. Stir in the soaked fruits, mixed peel, glacé cherries, glacé ginger and blanched almonds.

4. Sift together the flour and mixed spice, then fold lightly and evenly into the mixture. Spoon the mixture into the prepared tin and smooth the surface, making a slight depression in the centre with the back of the spoon.

5. Bake in the preheated oven for 2¼–2¾ hours, or until the cake is beginning to shrink away from the sides and a skewer inserted into the centre comes out clean. Leave in the tin to cool completely.

6. Wrap the cake in greaseproof paper and foil, and store for at least two months before use.

cals: 418   fat: 14.9g   sat fat: 8.1g   fibre: 3.4g   carbs: 71.1g   sugar: 50.4g   salt: 0.1g   protein: 5.3g

frosted carrot cake

prep: 55 mins, plus cooling
cook: 35 mins

150 g/5½ oz lightly salted butter, softened, plus extra for greasing

150 g/5½ oz light muscovado sugar

3 eggs, beaten

150 g/5½ oz self-raising flour

½ tsp baking powder

½ tsp ground mixed spice

85 g/3 oz ground almonds

finely grated rind of 1 lemon

150 g/5½ oz carrots, grated

85 g/3 oz sultanas, roughly chopped

frosting

150 g/5½ oz full-fat cream cheese

40 g/1½ oz unsalted butter, softened

115 g/4 oz icing sugar

2 tbsp lemon juice

decoration

60 g/2¼ oz marzipan

orange food colouring

several sprigs of fresh dill

1. Preheat the oven to 180°C/350°F/Gas Mark 4. Grease a 25 x 20-cm/10 x 8-inch baking tin and line with baking paper.

2. Put the butter, muscovado sugar, eggs, flour, baking powder, mixed spice, ground almonds and lemon rind in a mixing bowl and beat with a hand-held electric mixer until smooth and creamy. Stir in the carrots and sultanas.

3. Spoon the mixture into the prepared tin and smooth the surface. Bake in the preheated oven for 35 minutes, or until risen and just firm to the touch. Leave to cool in the tin for 10 minutes, then turn out onto a wire rack to cool completely.

4. For the frosting, beat together the cream cheese, butter, icing sugar and lemon juice until creamy.

5. Colour the marzipan deep orange by dotting a few drops of the food colouring onto the marzipan and kneading until the colour is evenly mixed. Roll the marzipan into a sausage shape, then divide it into 20 pieces. Form each piece into a small carrot shape, marking shallow grooves around it with a knife.

6. Using a palette knife, spread the frosting over the cake, taking it almost to the edges. Trim the crusts from the cake to neaten it, if necessary, then cut the cake into 20 squares.

7. Place a marzipan 'carrot' on top of each square and add a small sprig of dill for leaves.

top tip

To save time, look for carrot-shaped decorations in the cake decorating aisle of the supermarket.

serves 20

cals: 243   fat: 14.7g   sat fat: 7.1g   fibre: 1.2g   carbs: 25.7g   sugar: 17.7g   salt: 0.5g   protein: 3.7g

coffee bundt cake

prep: 45–50 mins, plus cooling
cook: 50 mins

400 g/14 oz plain flour, plus extra
  for dusting

1 tbsp baking powder

1 tsp bicarbonate of soda

3 tbsp espresso coffee powder

275 g/9¾ oz lightly salted butter,
  softened, plus extra for greasing

125 g/4½ oz light muscovado sugar

225 ml/8 fl oz maple syrup

3 eggs, beaten

225 ml/8 fl oz buttermilk

225 ml/8 fl oz double cream

decoration

4 tbsp maple syrup

200 g/7 oz icing sugar

15 g/½ oz unsalted butter, melted

20 milk, plain and white chocolate-
  coated coffee beans

1. Preheat the oven to 180°C/350°F/Gas Mark 4. Grease and lightly flour a 3-litre/5¼-pint Bundt tin.

2. Sift the flour, baking powder, bicarbonate of soda and coffee powder into a bowl. In a separate bowl, beat together the butter and muscovado sugar until pale and creamy. Gradually whisk in the maple syrup. Beat in the eggs slowly, adding 3 tablespoons of the flour mixture to prevent curdling.

3. Mix together the buttermilk and cream and add half to the butter mixture. Sprinkle in half of the flour mixture and fold gently together. Add the remaining buttermilk and flour mixtures and mix together gently until just combined.

4. Spoon the mixture into the prepared tin and smooth the surface. Bake in the preheated oven for about 50 minutes, or until well risen and a skewer inserted into the centre comes out clean. Leave to cool in the tin for 10 minutes, then loosen with a knife and turn out onto a wire rack to cool completely.

5. Beat the maple syrup in a bowl with 150 g/5½ oz of the icing sugar and the butter, until smooth and thickly coating the back of a wooden spoon. Transfer the cake to a serving plate and spoon the icing around the top of the cake so it starts to run down the sides.

6. Beat the remaining icing sugar in a small bowl with 1½–2 teaspoons of water to make a smooth paste. Using a teaspoon, drizzle the icing over the cake. Roughly chop the coffee beans, then scatter them over the top of the cake while the icing is still wet.

top tip

Bundt tins come in all sorts of shapes and designs. Make sure you use one with the correct capacity.

serves 14

cals: 510   fat: 27g   sat fat: 16.5g   fibre: 0.8g   carbs: 61.8g   sugar: 37.2g   salt: 1g   protein: 5.9g

dorset apple cake

prep: 30 mins, plus cooling
cook: 40 mins

2 eating apples, about 250 g/9 oz total weight

225 g/8 oz plain flour

1 tsp baking powder

125 g/4½ oz chilled unsalted butter, diced, plus extra for greasing

125 g/4½ oz caster sugar, plus extra for sprinkling

finely grated rind of 1 lemon

2 eggs, beaten

1. Preheat the oven to 190°C/375°F/Gas Mark 5. Lightly grease a 20-cm/8-inch round springform cake tin. Peel and core the apples, cut one of the apples into quarters lengthways, then thinly slice the quarters vertically and set aside. Dice the remaining apple and set aside.

2. Sift together the flour and baking powder into a large bowl. Add the butter and rub it in with your fingertips until the mixture resembles breadcrumbs.

3. Add the sugar, diced apple, lemon rind and eggs to the flour mixture and mix to a firm dough. Put into the prepared tin and prick several times with a fork. Decorate the top of the cake with the apple slices.

4. Bake in the preheated oven for 40 minutes. Remove from the oven and leave to cool for 1–2 minutes. Unclip and remove the sides, leaving the cake on the base of the tin, then transfer to a wire rack to cool completely. Sprinkle with sugar before serving.

top tip

This cake is especially delicious when served with softly whipped cream.

cals: 218   fat: 10.2g   sat fat: 6.1g   fibre: 1.1g   carbs: 27.8g   sugar: 13.5g   salt: 0.1g   protein: 3.3g

sticky toffee pudding

prep: 25 mins, plus soaking
cook: 40-45 mins

75 g/2¾ oz sultanas

150 g/5½ oz stoned dates, chopped

1 tsp bicarbonate of soda

25 g/1 oz unsalted butter, plus extra
   for greasing

200 g/7 oz soft light brown sugar

2 eggs

200 g/7 oz self-raising flour, sifted

grated rind of 1 orange, to decorate

sticky toffee sauce

25 g/1 oz butter

175 ml/6 fl oz double cream

200 g/7 oz soft light brown sugar

1. Put the sultanas, dates and bicarbonate of soda into a heatproof bowl. Cover with boiling water and leave to soak.

2. Preheat the oven to 180°C/350°F/Gas Mark 4. Grease a 20-cm/8-inch round cake tin.

3. Put the butter in a separate bowl, add the sugar and mix well. Beat in the eggs, then fold in the flour. Drain the soaked fruit, add to the bowl and mix. Spoon the mixture into the prepared tin.

4. Bake in the preheated oven for 35–40 minutes, or until a skewer inserted into the centre comes out clean.

5. About 5 minutes before the end of the cooking time, make the sauce. Melt the butter in a saucepan over a medium heat. Stir in the cream and sugar and bring to the boil, stirring constantly. Reduce the heat and simmer for 5 minutes.

6. Turn out the pudding onto a serving plate and pour over the sauce. Decorate with the grated orange rind.

cals: 533   fat: 18.1g   sat fat: 10.8g   fibre: 2.4g   carbs: 90.7g   sugar: 68.6g   salt: 1.2g   protein: 5.3g

coconut layer cake

prep: 40 mins, plus cooling
cook: 25–30 mins

6 large eggs, beaten

175 g/6 oz caster sugar

175 g/6 oz plain flour

70 g/2½ oz desiccated coconut

55 g/2 oz unsalted butter, melted and cooled, plus extra for greasing

toasted coconut shavings, to decorate

frosting

250 g/9 oz mascarpone cheese

4 tbsp coconut milk

25 g/1 oz caster sugar

150 ml/5 fl oz double cream

variation

For a fruity kick, try adding a layer of pineapple jam when you sandwich the cakes together.

1. Preheat the oven to 180°C/350°F/Gas Mark 4. Grease three 20-cm/8-inch round sandwich tins and line with baking paper.

2. Put the eggs and sugar into a large, heatproof bowl set over a saucepan of gently simmering water. Beat with a hand-held electric mixer until the mixture is thick and pale and leaves a trail when the beaters are lifted.

3. Sift in half of the flour and gently fold into the whisked mixture. Sift in the rest of the flour and fold in, followed by the desiccated coconut. Pour the butter in a thin stream over the mixture and fold in until just incorporated. Divide the mixture between the prepared tins.

4. Bake in the preheated oven for 20–25 minutes, or until light golden and springy to the touch. Leave to cool in the tins for 5 minutes, then turn out onto a wire rack to cool completely.

5. To make the frosting, put the mascarpone cheese, coconut milk and sugar into a bowl and beat together until smooth. Whip the cream until it holds soft peaks, then fold it into the mixture.

6. Sandwich the cakes together with one third of the frosting and spread the remainder over the top and sides of the cake. Decorate with coconut shavings.

serves 8

cals: 594 fat: 41.4g sat fat: 27.9g fibre: 2.2g carbs: 46.4g sugar: 27.9g salt: 0.2g protein: 10.5g

lining cake tins

Not all cake tins need to be fully lined before baking. For many simple sponges you simply need to give the base and sides of the tin a quick brush with oil or melted butter and maybe insert a piece of baking paper in the base. However, richer or low-fat mixtures usually need a thoroughly greased and lined tin to prevent the mixture from sticking to the tin.

Flouring tins

1. Grease the base and the sides of the tin or the indentations in the tin.

2. Sprinkle a little flour into the tin. Tilt the tin, tapping lightly so the flour coats the base and sides or the indentations evenly. Tip out any excess flour.

Lining a round tin

1. Grease the tin. Using scissors, cut a strip of baking paper about 2.5 cm/1 inch longer than the circumference of the tin and 2.5 cm/ 1 inch deeper.

2. Fold up one long side about 1 cm/½ inch from the edge, then unfold leaving a crease.

3. Snip cuts along the folded edge of the paper, then fit the paper into the sides of the tin.

4. Place the tin on a sheet of baking paper and draw around it with a pencil. Cut just inside the line to make a circle. Place into the base of the tin, covering the snipped edges of the side lining paper.

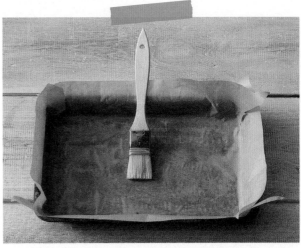

Lining a square tin

1. Grease the tin. Using scissors, cut a strip of baking paper about 2.5 cm/1 inch longer than the circumference of the tin and 2.5 cm/1 inch deeper.

2. Fold up one long side about 1 cm/½ inch from the edge, then unfold leaving a crease.

3. Fit the paper into the sides of the tin, cutting a diagonal slit into the folded edge to fit each corner.

4. Place the tin on a sheet of baking paper and draw around it with a pencil. Cut just inside the line to make a square. Place into the base of the tin, covering the folded edges of the side lining paper.

Lining a traybake or Swiss roll tin

1. Grease the tin. Using scissors, cut a piece of baking paper 7 cm/2¾ inches larger than the tin.

2. Place the tin on the paper, then make a cut from each corner of the paper towards the tin corner.

3. Place the paper inside the tin so that the diagonally cut corners overlap and fit neatly.

red velvet cake

prep: 25-30 mins, plus cooling
cook: 30-35 mins

225 g/8 oz unsalted butter,
  plus extra for greasing
4 tbsp water
55 g/2 oz cocoa powder
3 eggs, beaten
250 ml/9 fl oz buttermilk
2 tsp vanilla extract
2 tbsp red food colouring
280 g/10 oz plain flour
55 g/2 oz cornflour
1½ tsp baking powder
280 g/10 oz caster sugar

frosting
250 g/9 oz cream cheese
40 g/1½ oz unsalted butter
3 tbsp caster sugar
1 tsp vanilla extract

top tip

To make your own buttermilk, put 250 ml/
9 fl oz milk in a jug and stir in 1 tablespoon
of lemon juice or white wine vinegar. Leave to
stand for 5 minutes before using.

1. Preheat the oven to 190°C/375°F/Gas
Mark 5. Grease two 23-cm/9-inch sandwich
tins and line with baking paper.

2. Place the butter, water and cocoa powder
in a small saucepan and heat gently,
without boiling, stirring until melted and
smooth. Remove from the heat and leave
to cool slightly.

3. Beat together the eggs, buttermilk, vanilla
extract and food colouring in a bowl. Beat in
the butter mixture. Sift together the flour,
cornflour and baking powder, then stir into
the mixture with the caster sugar.

4. Divide the mixture between the prepared
tins and bake in the preheated oven for
25–30 minutes, or until risen and firm to
the touch. Leave to cool in the tins for
3–4 minutes, then turn out onto a wire rack
to cool completely.

5. To make the frosting, beat together all the
ingredients until smooth. Use about half of
the frosting to sandwich the cakes together,
then spread the remainder over the top.

cals: 487   fat: 28.3g   sat fat: 16.9g   fibre: 2.2g   carbs: 53.6g   sugar: 29.2g   salt: 0.4g   protein: 7.3g

hot chocolate fudge layer cake

prep: 30-35 mins, plus cooling
cook: 8-10 mins

unsalted butter, for greasing

3 eggs

85 g/3 oz caster sugar,
  plus extra for sprinkling

85 g/3 oz plain flour

2 tbsp cocoa powder,
  plus extra for dusting

200 ml/7 fl oz double cream

225 g/8 oz ready-made chocolate
  fudge frosting

plain and white chocolate curls,
  to decorate

1. Preheat the oven to 200°C/400°F/Gas Mark 6. Grease a 33 x 23-cm/13 x 9-inch Swiss roll tin and line with baking paper.

2. Put the eggs and sugar into a large bowl set over a saucepan of gently simmering water. Whisk with a hand-held electric mixer for 3–4 minutes, or until the mixture is very thick and pale.

3. Sift in the flour and cocoa powder and gently fold in. Pour into the prepared tin and level the surface. Bake in the preheated oven for 8–10 minutes, or until risen and springy to the touch. Meanwhile, dust a chopping board with caster sugar and whip the cream until it holds firm peaks.

4. Remove the cake from the oven and turn out onto the prepared board. Cut into three strips and transfer to a wire rack to cool slightly. Spread a third of the frosting over the top of each strip and sandwich together with the whipped cream. Decorate with chocolate curls, dust with cocoa and serve warm.

top tip

In step 2, the mixture should be thick enough to leave a ribbon-like trail when the beaters are lifted.

cals: 364   fat: 20.4g   sat fat: 11.6g   fibre: 1.7g   carbs: 40.4g   sugar: 29.9g   salt: 0.3g   protein: 5.2g

polenta & blueberry loaf cake

prep: 20-25 mins, plus cooling
cook: 40-45 mins

150 g/5½ oz unsalted butter, softened,
   plus extra for greasing
225 g/8 oz caster sugar
3 eggs, beaten
150 g/5½ oz polenta
100 g/3½ oz ground almonds
2 tsp baking powder
150 g/5½ oz blueberries
finely grated rind and juice of 1 lemon

fact

This deliciously moist cake is gluten-free.
It uses polenta, which is finely ground corn,
and ground almonds instead of wheat flour.

1. Preheat the oven to 180°C/350°F/Gas
Mark 4. Grease a 900-g/2-lb loaf tin and line
with baking paper.

2. Cream the butter with 175 g/6 oz of the
sugar until pale, light and fluffy. Add the
eggs, polenta, ground almonds and baking
powder, and gently beat to combine. Fold in
the blueberries and lemon rind, then pour
the mixture into the prepared tin.

3. Bake in the preheated oven for
35–40 minutes, until risen and golden brown.

4. Put the remaining sugar in a saucepan
with the lemon juice. Bring to the boil and
boil for 1–2 minutes, until it is thickened
and syrupy.

5. Remove the cake from the oven and leave
in the tin. Pierce the surface all over with a
cocktail stick and pour the syrup over the
cake. Leave to cool completely before turning
out of the tin.

cals: 350   fat: 20.1g   sat fat: 9.1g   fibre: 2g   carbs: 39g   sugar: 24.9g   salt: 0.3g   protein: 5.6g

pumpkin spice cake

prep: 30 mins, plus cooling
cook: 35-40 mins

175 ml/6 fl oz sunflower oil,
    plus extra for greasing
175 g/6 oz soft light brown sugar
3 eggs, beaten
250 g/9 oz canned pumpkin purée
85 g/3 oz raisins
grated rind of 1 orange
70 g/2½ oz walnut pieces
225 g/8 oz self-raising flour
1 tsp bicarbonate of soda
2 tsp ground mixed spice

frosting
250 g/9 oz mascarpone cheese
85 g/3 oz icing sugar
3 tbsp maple syrup

1. Preheat the oven to 180°C/350°F/Gas Mark 4. Grease a 23-cm/9-inch square cake tin and line with baking paper.

2. In a large bowl, beat together the oil, brown sugar and eggs. Stir in the pumpkin purée, raisins, orange rind and 55 g/2 oz of the walnut pieces.

3. Sift together the flour, bicarbonate of soda and mixed spice and fold into the pumpkin mixture. Spoon into the prepared tin.

4. Bake in the preheated oven for 35–40 minutes, or until golden brown and firm to the touch. Leave to cool in the tin for 5 minutes, then turn out onto a wire rack to cool completely.

5. To make the frosting, put the mascarpone cheese, icing sugar and maple syrup into a bowl and beat together until smooth. Spread over the top of the cake, swirling with a palette knife. Finely chop the remaining walnut pieces and scatter over the top.

cals: 630   fat: 39.4g   sat fat: 11.7g   fibre: 2.5g   carbs: 64.7g   sugar: 41.2g   salt: 1.2g   protein: 7.7g

raspberry & almond cake

prep: 25 mins, plus cooling
cook: 22-25 mins

115 g/4 oz self-raising flour

¼ tsp baking powder

2 eggs

115 g/4 oz unsalted butter, softened, plus extra for greasing

115 g/4 oz caster sugar

40 g/1½ oz ground almonds

175 g/6 oz raspberries

2 tbsp flaked almonds

icing sugar, for dusting

1. Preheat the oven to 200°C/400°F/Gas Mark 6. Place a baking sheet in the oven to preheat. Grease a 23-cm/9-inch round cake tin and line the base with baking paper.

2. Sift together the flour and baking powder into a large bowl. Add the eggs, butter and caster sugar and beat with a hand-held electric mixer for 1–2 minutes, until pale and creamy. Fold in the ground almonds.

3. Spoon the mixture into the prepared tin. Gently level the surface and scatter over the raspberries and flaked almonds. Bake in the preheated oven for 22–25 minutes, or until risen, golden brown and just firm to the touch.

4. Leave to cool in the tin for 1–2 minutes, then turn out onto a wire rack. Dust with icing sugar and serve warm or cold.

variation

Experiment with using different fruits, such as apricots, in this cake instead of the raspberries.

cals: 248   fat: 18.2g   sat fat: 8.8g   fibre: 2.6g   carbs: 30.2g   sugar: 17g   salt: 0.5g   protein: 5.2g

soured cream cake with nectarines

prep: 30 mins, plus cooling
cook: 1 hour 5 mins

unsalted butter, for greasing

40 g/1½ oz dried breadcrumbs

3 nectarines

750 g/1 lb 10 oz low-fat curd cheese or quark

100 ml/3½ fl oz soured cream

3 eggs

150 g/5½ oz caster sugar

1 sachet vanilla blancmange powder

100 ml/3½ fl oz sunflower oil

100 ml/3½ fl oz milk

50 g/1¾ oz ground almonds

icing sugar, for dusting

1. Preheat the oven to 160°C/325°F/Gas Mark 3. Grease a 26-cm/10½-inch round springform cake tin and sprinkle the base and sides with the breadcrumbs.

2. Stone the nectarines, then cut them into thin slices.

3. Put the curd cheese into a mixing bowl with the soured cream, eggs, caster sugar, blancmange powder, oil, milk and ground almonds, and beat with a hand-held electric mixer until smooth and creamy.

4. Spoon the mixture into the prepared tin and arrange the nectarine slices in a circle on top. Bake in the preheated oven for 1 hour 5 minutes.

5. Leave to cool in the tin, then carefully turn out of the tin and transfer to a cake plate. Dust with icing sugar just before serving.

fact

Quark is a soft curd cheese popular in Europe, especially in German-speaking countries. It is widely available in large supermarkets.

cals: 332   fat: 17.8g   sat fat: 3.7g   fibre: 1.4g   carbs: 31.3g   sugar: 23.5g   salt: 0.3g   protein: 13.4g

cookie ice-cream cake

prep: 40-45 mins, plus chilling and freezing
cook: 15 mins

175 g/6 oz unsalted butter, softened,
  plus extra for greasing
200 g/7 oz soft dark brown sugar
100 g/3½ oz caster sugar
1 egg
1 egg yolk
1 tsp vanilla extract
250 g/9 oz plain flour
½ tsp salt
½ tsp bicarbonate of soda
325 g/11½ oz plain chocolate,
  broken into small pieces
2 litres/3½ pints vanilla ice cream

1. Using a food processor on high, cream together the butter and sugars until pale and doubled in size – this will take approximately 8 minutes. Reduce the speed of the food processor slightly and gradually add the egg, egg yolk and vanilla extract until well combined. Turn off the food processor and sift in the flour, salt and bicarbonate of soda. With the food processor on low, process the mixture until well combined, then add the chocolate pieces and mix briefly. Place the dough in the refrigerator for 30 minutes.

2. Preheat the oven to 180°C/350°F/Gas Mark 4. Grease three 23-cm/9-inch round cake tins and line with baking paper.

3. Remove the dough from the refrigerator and divide into three equal-sized pieces. Press the dough into the bottom of the prepared tins, making sure the dough is even and goes right to the edges.

4. Bake in the preheated oven for 15 minutes, or until just turning golden. Leave to cool in the tins.

5. Meanwhile, remove the ice cream from the freezer and allow to soften.

6. Remove two of the cookies from their tins. Keep the third cookie in its tin as the cake base and build your cake with alternate, equal-sized layers of ice cream and cookie, finishing with the final – and best-looking – cookie on top. Push down gently to make sure the ice cream comes to the sides of the tin. Place in the freezer for 4 hours before serving.

top tip

Remove this cake from the freezer 10 minutes before serving to make it easier to cut.

serves 10

cals: 911   fat: 44.5g   sat fat: 28.8g   fibre: 5.4g   carbs: 115.4g   sugar: 84.2g   salt: 0.7g   protein: 12.2g

piñata party cake

prep: 50-55 mins, plus cooling and chilling
cook: 1¼ hours-1 hour 25 mins

450 g/1 lb unsalted butter, softened,
  plus extra for greasing

450 g/1 lb caster sugar

8 large eggs, beaten

450 g/1 lb self-raising flour

115 g/4 oz plain flour

4 tbsp milk

frosting

100 g/3½ oz white chocolate, broken
  into pieces

200 g/7 oz butter, softened

400 g/14 oz icing sugar, sifted

filling and decoration

280 g/10 oz mixed sweets, such as jelly
  babies, jelly beans and sugar-coated
  chocolate drops

2 tbsp pastel-coloured confetti sugar
  sprinkles

1. Preheat the oven to 160°C/325°F/Gas
Mark 3. Grease two 2-litre/3½-pint ovenproof
bowls.

2. Put the butter and sugar into a large bowl
and beat with a hand-held electric mixer
until pale and creamy. Gradually beat in the
eggs a little at a time. Sift together the flours,
then fold into the creamed mixture with the
milk. Divide the mixture evenly between the
prepared bowls, making a dip in the centre.

3. Bake in the preheated oven for 50 minutes,
then loosely cover each bowl with foil and
bake for a further 20–30 minutes, or until
firm to the touch and a skewer inserted in the
centre of the cakes comes out clean. Leave
to cool in the bowls for 10 minutes, then
turn out onto a wire rack to cool completely.
Wrap the cold cakes in foil and chill in the
refrigerator for 4–5 hours, or overnight.

4. To make the frosting, put the chocolate
in a heatproof bowl set over a saucepan of
gently simmering water and heat until melted.
Remove from the heat and leave to cool for
15 minutes. Put the butter into a large bowl
and gradually beat in the sugar, then beat in
the melted chocolate.

5. To assemble, level the top of each cake with a serrated knife. Scoop out the centres of the cakes, leaving a 4-cm/1½-inch border. Place one cake, cut-side up, on a serving plate. Spread some of the frosting around the rim of the cake and pile the sweets and half the sprinkles into the centre. Invert the second cake on top to enclose the sweets and make a globe-shaped cake, pressing down gently.

6. Using a palette knife, spread a thin layer of frosting all over the cake to secure any loose crumbs, then chill in the refrigerator for 1 hour. Spread the remaining frosting in a thick layer over the cake and decorate with the remaining sprinkles.

serves 12

cals: 1043   fat: 53.9g   sat fat: 32.5g   fibre: 1.4g   carbs: 130.5g   sugar: 94.1g   salt: 1g   protein: 12g

treat yourself!

There's an old saying that a little bit of what you fancy does you good, and this is definitely the case when it comes to baked goodies! The tasty treats in this chapter include cookies, cupcakes, muffins, and whoopie pies — all in perfectly portion-sized packages, making it easy for you to watch your waistline whilst still indulging.

a bit of what you fancy

chocolate chip cookies → 46

apple streusel cupcakes → 48

rocky road chocolate muffins → 50

luscious lemon whoopie pies → 52

jam rings → 54

blondies → 56

summer garden cupcakes → 58

chocolate caramel squares → 60

red velvet crinkle cookies → 62

BASIC TECHNIQUES → 64

strawberry & cream whoopie pies → 66

chocolate pretzel fudge squares → 68

raspberry crumble muffins → 70

cake pops → 72

blueberry cheesecake bars → 74

fluffy gingerbread cupcakes → 76

raisin flapjacks → 78

chocolate chip cookies

prep: 15–20 mins, plus cooling
cook: 15–17 mins

175 g/6 oz plain flour, sifted

1 tsp baking powder

125 g/4½ oz margarine, melted, plus extra for greasing

85 g/3 oz light muscovado sugar

55 g/2 oz caster sugar

½ tsp vanilla extract

1 egg, beaten

125 g/4½ oz plain chocolate chips

1. Preheat the oven to 190°C/375°F/Gas Mark 5. Grease two baking sheets.

2. Place all the ingredients in a large mixing bowl and beat until well combined.

3. Place tablespoons of the mixture on the prepared baking sheets, spaced well apart.

4. Bake in the preheated oven for 10–12 minutes, or until golden brown. Transfer to a wire rack and leave to cool.

variation

Add some roughly chopped nuts to the cookie mixture — try pecan nuts, hazelnuts or almonds.

cals: 355   fat: 18.8g   sat fat: 6.7g   fibre: 1.8g   carbs: 42.5g   sugar: 23.4g   salt: 0.3g   protein: 4.1g

apple streusel cupcakes

prep: 25-30 mins, plus cooling
cook: 18-20 mins

½ tsp bicarbonate of soda
280 g/10 oz apple sauce (from a jar)
55 g/2 oz unsalted butter, softened
85 g/3 oz demerara sugar
1 large egg, lightly beaten
175 g/6 oz self-raising flour
½ tsp ground cinnamon
½ tsp freshly grated nutmeg

topping
50 g/1¾ oz plain flour
50 g/1¾ oz demerara sugar
¼ tsp ground cinnamon
¼ tsp freshly grated nutmeg
35 g/1¼ oz unsalted butter, diced

1. Preheat the oven to 180°C/350°F/Gas Mark 4. Line two bun tins with 14 paper cases. To make the topping, put the flour, sugar and spices in a bowl. Rub in the butter until the mixture resembles fine breadcrumbs.

2. Add the bicarbonate of soda to the apple sauce and stir until dissolved. Place the butter and sugar in a large bowl and beat until light and fluffy. Add the egg, then sift in the flour, cinnamon and nutmeg and fold into the mixture, adding the apple sauce mixture a spoonful at a time.

3. Spoon the mixture into the paper cases. Scatter the topping over the cupcakes and press down gently. Bake in the preheated oven for 18–20 minutes, or until risen, golden and firm to the touch. Transfer to a wire rack and leave to cool completely.

top tip

You can freeze the cupcakes for up to two months packed into a freezer box.

rocky road
chocolate muffins

225 g/8 oz plain flour

55 g/2 oz cocoa powder

1 tbsp baking powder

pinch of salt

115 g/4 oz caster sugar

100 g/3½ oz white chocolate chips

50 g/1¾ oz white mini marshmallows, cut in half

2 eggs

250 ml/9 fl oz milk

6 tbsp sunflower oil or 85 g/3 oz butter, melted and cooled, plus extra for greasing (if using)

1. Preheat the oven to 200°C/400°F/Gas Mark 6. Grease a 12-hole muffin tin or line with 12 paper cases. Sift together the flour, cocoa, baking powder and salt into a large bowl. Stir in the sugar, chocolate chips and marshmallows.

2. Lightly beat the eggs in a large jug or bowl, then beat in the milk and oil. Make a well in the centre of the dry ingredients and pour in the beaten liquid ingredients. Stir gently until just combined; do not over-mix.

3. Spoon the mixture into the prepared muffin tin. Bake in the preheated oven for about 20 minutes, until risen and firm to the touch.

4. Leave the muffins to cool in the tin for 5 minutes, then serve warm or transfer to a wire rack to cool completely.

top tip

When making muffins, it's important not to over-work the mixture. Take care to stir it until the ingredients are only just combined in step 2.

makes 12

cals: 263   fat: 11.9g   sat fat: 3.4g   fibre: 2g   carbs: 35.8g   sugar: 18.1g   salt: 0.7g   protein: 5.4g

luscious lemon whoopie pies

prep: 40-45 mins, plus cooling
cook: 20-24 mins

250 g/9 oz plain flour

2 tsp baking powder

large pinch of salt

115 g/4 oz unsalted butter, softened

150 g/5½ oz caster sugar

finely grated rind of 1 lemon

1 large egg, beaten

100 ml/3½ fl oz milk

4 tbsp lemon curd

2 tbsp yellow sugar sprinkles,
  to decorate

lemon buttercream

115 g/4 oz unsalted butter, softened

2 tbsp lemon juice

200 g/7 oz icing sugar, sifted

icing

115 g/4 oz icing sugar

1–2 tbsp warm water

1. Preheat the oven to 180°C/350°F/Gas Mark 4. Line two large baking sheets with baking paper. Sift together the flour, baking powder and salt.

2. Place the butter, caster sugar and lemon rind in a large bowl and beat with a hand-held electric mixer until pale and fluffy.

Beat in the egg followed by half the flour mixture and then the milk. Stir in the rest of the flour mixture and mix until thoroughly incorporated.

3. Pipe or spoon 20 mounds of the mixture onto the prepared baking sheets, spaced well apart. Bake in the preheated oven, one sheet at a time, for 10–12 minutes, until risen and just firm to the touch. Leave to cool for 5 minutes, then transfer to a wire rack to cool completely.

4. For the buttercream, place the butter and lemon juice in a bowl and beat with a hand-held electric mixer for 2–3 minutes, until pale and creamy. Gradually beat in the icing sugar and continue beating for 2–3 minutes, until the buttercream is very light and fluffy.

5. For the icing, sift the icing sugar into a bowl and gradually stir in enough water to make a smooth icing that is thick enough to coat the back of a wooden spoon.

6. To assemble, spread the buttercream on the flat side of half of the cakes and the lemon curd over the other half of the cakes. Sandwich the cakes together. Spoon the icing over the whoopie pies and decorate with the sprinkles.

cals: 473   fat: 19.7g   sat fat: 12.1g   fibre: 0.8g   carbs: 71.4g   sugar: 52.2g   salt: 0.6g   protein: 3.9g

jam rings

prep: 40-45 mins, plus chilling and cooling
cook: 12-15 mins

225 g/8 oz unsalted butter, softened

140 g/5 oz caster sugar, plus extra
  for sprinkling

1 egg yolk, lightly beaten

2 tsp vanilla extract

280 g/10 oz plain flour

pinch of salt

1 egg white, lightly beaten

filling

55 g/2 oz unsalted butter, softened

100 g/3½ oz icing sugar

5 tbsp strawberry or raspberry jam

1. Put the butter and caster sugar into a bowl and mix well with a wooden spoon, then beat in the egg yolk and vanilla extract. Sift the flour and salt into the mixture and stir until thoroughly combined. Halve the dough and shape into balls, then wrap in clingfilm and chill in the refrigerator for 30–60 minutes.

2. Preheat the oven to 190°C/375°F/Gas Mark 5. Line two baking sheets with baking paper.

3. Unwrap the dough and roll out between two sheets of baking paper. Stamp out 30 cookies with a 7-cm/2¾-inch fluted round cutter and put half of them on one of the prepared baking sheets, spaced well apart. Using a 4-cm/1½-inch plain round cutter, stamp out the centres of the remaining cookies and remove. Put the cookie rings on the other baking sheet, spaced well apart.

4. Bake in the preheated oven for 7 minutes, then brush the cookie rings with beaten egg white and sprinkle with caster sugar. Bake for a further 5–8 minutes, until light golden brown. Leave to cool on the baking sheets for 5–10 minutes, then carefully transfer to wire racks to cool completely.

5. Beat together the butter and icing sugar in a bowl until smooth and combined. Spread the buttercream over the whole cookies and top with a little of the jam. Place the cookie rings on top and press gently together.

makes 15

cals: 283   fat: 15.7g   sat fat: 9.7g   fibre: 0.6g   carbs: 33.2g   sugar: 18.6g   salt: 0.2g   protein: 2.8g

blondies

prep: 20 mins, plus cooling
cook: 25–27 mins

115 g/4 oz unsalted butter, plus extra for greasing

225 g/8 oz light muscovado sugar

2 eggs

1 tsp vanilla extract

150 g/5½ oz plain flour

pinch of salt

85 g/3 oz white chocolate chunks or chips

1. Preheat the oven to 200°C/400°F/Gas Mark 6. Grease a 20-cm/8-inch square cake tin and line with baking paper.

2. Put the butter into a small saucepan and melt over a low heat. Transfer to a large bowl with the sugar, then beat with a balloon whisk.

3. Beat in the eggs and vanilla extract, then sift in the flour and salt and beat well until smooth. Pour the mixture into the prepared tin and level the surface with a spatula. Scatter over the chocolate chunks.

4. Bake in the preheated oven for 20–22 minutes, or until golden brown and just set. Leave to cool in the tin.

makes 16

top tip

Just like brownies, blondies should remain a little soft and gooey in the centre when cooked.

cals: 184   fat: 8.8g   sat fat: 5.3g   fibre: 0.3g   carbs: 24.4g   sugar: 17.3g   salt: 0.2g   protein: 2.2g

summer garden cupcakes

prep: 50 mins, plus cooling
cook: 15–20 mins

115 g/4 oz unsalted butter, softened, or soft margarine

115 g/4 oz caster sugar

2 tsp rosewater

2 large eggs, lightly beaten

115 g/4 oz self-raising flour

decoration

115 g/4 oz pink ready-to-roll fondant icing

85 g/3 oz white ready-to-roll fondant icing

85 g/3 oz blue ready-to-roll fondant icing

yellow writing icing

buttercream

175 g/6 oz unsalted butter, softened

6 tbsp double cream

350 g/12 oz icing sugar

green food colouring

1. Preheat the oven to 180°C/350°F/Gas Mark 4. Line a 12-hole muffin tin with eight paper cases.

2. Place the butter, caster sugar and rosewater in a large bowl and beat together until light and fluffy. Gradually beat in the eggs. Sift in the flour and, using a metal spoon, fold in gently.

3. Spoon the mixture into the paper cases. Bake in the preheated oven for 15–20 minutes, or until risen, golden and firm to the touch. Transfer to a wire rack and leave to cool.

4. For the decoration, roll out the pink fondant icing to a thickness of 5 mm/¼ inch. Using a small butterfly cutter, stamp out 16 butterflies. Roll out the white and blue fondant icings to the same thickness and, using a small daisy cutter, stamp out about 40 flowers, re-rolling the icing as necessary. Use the yellow writing icing to pipe centres in the flowers.

5. For the buttercream, place the butter in a bowl and beat with a hand-held electric mixer for 2–3 minutes, until pale and creamy. Beat in the cream, then gradually sift in the icing sugar and continue beating for 2–3 minutes, until light and fluffy. Beat in a little green food colouring to give a light green colour.

6. Spoon the buttercream into a large piping bag fitted with a large star nozzle. Pipe swirls of buttercream on top of each cupcake. Decorate with the fondant butterflies and flowers.

top tip

Most supermarkets stock a range of edible cake decorations should you wish to take a short-cut

makes 8

cals: 762   fat: 38.8g   sat fat: 23.8g   fibre: 0.6g   carbs: 102.2g   sugar: 90g   salt: 0.5g   protein: 3.9g

chocolate caramel squares

prep: 25-30 mins, plus cooling and setting
cook: 40-45 mins

75 g/2¾ oz margarine, plus extra
  for greasing
60 g/2¼ oz soft light brown sugar
140 g/5 oz plain flour
40 g/1½ oz rolled oats

caramel filling
30 g/1 oz unsalted butter
2 tbsp soft light brown sugar
225 g/8 oz condensed milk

topping
100 g/3½ oz plain chocolate, broken
  into pieces
25 g/1 oz white chocolate, broken into
  pieces

top tip

To save time, you can always use a tin of ready-made caramel for the filling instead of making your own.

1. Preheat the oven to 180°C/350°F/Gas Mark 4. Grease a 20-cm/8-inch square cake tin.

2. Beat together the margarine and sugar in a bowl until light and fluffy. Beat in the flour and the rolled oats. Use your fingertips to bring the mixture together, if necessary. Press the mixture into the base of the prepared tin.

3. Bake in the preheated oven for 25 minutes, or until light golden. Leave to cool in the tin.

4. Place the ingredients for the caramel filling in a saucepan and heat gently, stirring until the sugar has dissolved. Bring slowly to the boil over a very low heat, then boil very gently for 3–4 minutes, stirring constantly, until thickened. Pour the caramel filling over the oat layer in the tin and leave to set.

5. Place the plain chocolate in a heatproof bowl set over a saucepan of gently simmering water and heat until melted. Spread the melted chocolate over the caramel layer. Leave to set.

6. Melt the white chocolate as described above. Spoon into a piping bag, then pipe lines of white chocolate over the plain chocolate. Using a cocktail stick, feather the white chocolate into the plain chocolate. Leave to set, then cut into squares.

cals: 200   fat: 9.5g   sat fat: 4.4g   fibre: 1g   carbs: 26.1g   sugar: 16.8g   salt: 0.1g   protein: 2.9g

red velvet crinkle cookies

prep: 30 mins, plus chilling and cooling
cook: 14–16 mins

115 g/4 oz unsalted butter, softened

200 g/7 oz light muscovado sugar

2 eggs, beaten

2 tsp red food colouring

280 g/10 oz plain flour

¼ tsp bicarbonate of soda

1 tsp baking powder

40 g/1½ oz cocoa powder

25 g/1 oz icing sugar

1. Put the butter and muscovado sugar into a large bowl and beat with a hand-held electric mixer until pale and fluffy. Gradually beat in the eggs, then the food colouring.

2. Sift the flour, bicarbonate of soda, baking powder and cocoa into the mixture. Stir with a wooden spoon to make a soft dough.

3. Cover and chill in the refrigerator for 30–40 minutes, or until the dough is firm enough to shape.

4. Preheat the oven to 190°C/375°F/Gas Mark 5. Line two large baking sheets with baking paper.

5. Divide the dough into 22 pieces, then shape each into a ball. Sift the icing sugar onto a plate. Roll each ball of dough in the icing sugar to coat, then place on the prepared baking sheets. Flatten to form 6-cm/2½-inch rounds.

6. Bake in the preheated oven for 14–16 minutes, or until just set. Leave to cool on the baking sheets for 5 minutes, then transfer to a wire rack to cool completely. Sprinkle any remaining icing sugar over the cookies.

top tip

These colourful cookies are best
eaten on the day of making.

cals: 134   fat: 5.1g   sat fat: 3g   fibre: 0.9g   carbs: 20.9g   sugar: 10.3g   salt: 0.1g   protein: 2.3g

basic techniques

Here are some of the basic baking methods that you will come across in the recipes in this book. It might take a little time and practice, but it is essential to master these techniques if you want to become a proficient baker.

Creaming

Butter and sugar are beaten together thoroughly to form a light, pale and fluffy mixture. It's essential that the butter is a soft, spreadable consistency before you start – but not melted. Use a wooden spoon or an electric mixer on a low speed and take care not to over-beat or the mixture will become oily.

Adding eggs

With many recipes, whole eggs should be beaten before gradually adding them to creamed and other mixtures. Beat well after each addition and, if the mixture begins to curdle, add a couple of spoonfuls of the measured flour before adding more eggs.

Sifting

Always sift the flour with any raising agents or ground spices before adding to a mixture so that they are evenly distributed.

Folding in

When folding in flour or dry ingredients, use a large metal spoon to gently cut and fold it through the creamed mixture. Don't use a wooden spoon or beat the mixture as this will knock out air bubbles and produce a close-textured cake.

Whisking

To make whisked sponge batters or egg white-based dishes, including meringues or macaroons, large amounts of air need to be incorporated and trapped in the mixture. Use an electric hand-held mixer for speed, or use a balloon whisk and plenty of elbow grease!

Rubbing in

This technique is used for pastries, scones, biscuits and some cakes. The fat (usually butter) needs to be chilled and diced or coarsely grated before rubbing into the flour. Make sure your hands are clean and cold and rub the fat into the flour between the tips of your fingers until it resembles fine breadcrumbs. Occasionally shake the bowl to bring any large lumps of fat to the surface.

Kneading

The stretching, folding and pushing of bread dough with floured hands is a vital technique that strengthens the dough and makes it more elastic. This in turn helps the dough to rise. It will take 5–10 minutes of kneading to achieve a smooth and elastic dough.

Melting chocolate

Break the chocolate into a large, heatproof bowl. Set the bowl over a pan of simmering water, making sure the bowl does not touch the water, and leave until the chocolate has melted, stirring occasionally. Remove the bowl from the pan and stir until smooth. Take care to avoid getting drips of water or condensation into the bowl as this will cause the chocolate to 'seize' and become grainy.

Baking blind

This technique is used to partially or fully bake a pastry case before adding a filling. Line the pastry case with baking paper and weigh down with ceramic baking beans or dried pulses (this prevents the pastry from rising), then bake as the recipe instructs.

strawberry & cream whoopie pies

prep: 40 mins, plus cooling
cook: 30-36 mins

250 g/9 oz plain flour
1 tsp bicarbonate of soda
large pinch of salt
115 g/4 oz unsalted butter, softened
150 g/5½ oz caster sugar
1 large egg, beaten
2 tsp rosewater
150 ml/5 fl oz buttermilk
icing sugar, for dusting

filling

300 ml/10 fl oz double cream
4 tbsp icing sugar, sifted
3 tbsp strawberry conserve
225 g/8 oz strawberries,
   hulled and sliced

top tip

Piping the mixture onto the baking sheets in step 3 will ensure even-sized and shaped rounds, but using a tablespoon or small ice-cream scoop will work well too.

1. Preheat the oven to 180°C/350°F/Gas Mark 4. Line two or three large baking sheets with baking paper. Sift together the flour, bicarbonate of soda and salt.

2. Place the butter and caster sugar in a large bowl and beat with a hand-held electric mixer until pale and fluffy. Beat in the egg and rosewater followed by half the flour mixture and then the buttermilk. Stir in the rest of the flour mixture and mix until thoroughly incorporated.

3. Pipe or spoon 24 mounds of the mixture onto the prepared baking sheets, spaced well apart. Bake in the preheated oven, one sheet at a time, for 10–12 minutes, until risen and just firm to the touch. Leave to cool for 5 minutes, then transfer to a wire rack to cool completely.

4. For the filling, place the cream in a bowl and whip until holding firm peaks. Fold in the icing sugar.

5. To assemble, spread the strawberry conserve on the flat side of half of the cakes, followed by the whipped cream and strawberries. Top with the remaining cakes and press together lightly. Dust with icing sugar.

makes 12

cals: 357   fat: 20.7g   sat fat: 12.7g   fibre: 1g   carbs: 39.5g   sugar: 22.6g   salt: 0.6g   protein: 3.9g

chocolate pretzel fudge squares

prep: 20 mins, plus cooling and chilling
cook: 8-10 mins

sunflower oil, for greasing
175 g/6 oz mini pretzels
25 g/1 oz unsalted butter, diced
300 g/10½ oz milk chocolate chips
400 g/14 oz condensed milk
1 tsp vanilla extract

1. Lightly brush a 24-cm/9½-inch square cake tin with oil and line with baking paper. Roughly chop 55 g/2 oz of the pretzels.

2. Put the butter, chocolate chips, condensed milk and vanilla extract in a heatproof bowl set over a saucepan of gently simmering water and heat, stirring occasionally, for 8–10 minutes, or until the chocolate has just melted and the mixture is smooth and warm but not hot. Remove from the heat and stir in the chopped pretzels.

3. Pour the mixture into the prepared tin, smooth the surface using a spatula and push in the whole pretzels. Leave to cool for 1 hour. Cover with clingfilm, then chill in the refrigerator for 1–2 hours, or until firm.

4. Lift the fudge out of the tin and cut it into 16 squares.

top tip

This fudge can be stored in an airtight container in a cool, dry place for up to two weeks.

raspberry crumble muffins

prep: 25-30 mins, plus cooling
cook: 25 mins

280 g/10 oz plain flour
1 tbsp baking powder
½ tsp bicarbonate of soda
pinch of salt
115 g/4 oz caster sugar
2 eggs
250 ml/9 fl oz natural yogurt
85 g/3 oz unsalted butter, melted
  and cooled
1 tsp vanilla extract
150 g/5½ oz frozen raspberries

crumble topping
50 g/1¾ oz plain flour
35 g/1¼ oz unsalted butter
25 g/1 oz caster sugar

variation

For raspberry and blueberry crumble muffins, simply substitute blueberries for half the raspberries in this recipe.

1. Preheat the oven to 200°C/400°F/Gas Mark 6. Line a 12-hole muffin tin with 12 paper cases.

2. To make the crumble topping, sift the flour into a bowl. Cut the butter into small pieces, add to the bowl with the flour and rub it in with your fingertips until the mixture resembles fine breadcrumbs. Stir in the sugar and set aside.

3. To make the muffins, sift together the flour, baking powder, bicarbonate of soda and salt into a large bowl. Stir in the sugar.

4. Lightly beat the eggs in a large bowl, then beat in the yogurt, melted butter and vanilla extract. Make a well in the centre of the dry ingredients, pour in the beaten liquid ingredients and add the raspberries. Stir gently until just combined; do not over-mix.

5. Spoon the mixture into the paper cases. Scatter the crumble topping over the muffins and press down lightly. Bake in the preheated oven for about 20 minutes, until well risen, golden brown and firm to the touch.

6. Leave the muffins to cool in the tin for 5 minutes, then serve warm or transfer to a wire rack to cool completely.

makes 12

cals: 251   fat: 10g   sat fat: 5.9g   fibre: 1.5g   carbs: 35g   sugar: 13.3g   salt: 0.8g   protein: 4.9g

cake pops

175 g/6 oz ready-made sponge cake
(vanilla or chocolate flavour)

70 g/2½ oz ready-made chocolate
fudge frosting, at room temperature

175 g/6 oz yellow or pink candy melts

about 30 g/1 oz star- and polka-dot-
shaped sugar sprinkles, to decorate

8 cake pop sticks

1. Crumble the sponge cake into a bowl.
Add the frosting and beat with a wooden
spoon until thoroughly mixed.

2. Use your hands to divide and shape the
mixture into eight firm, walnut-sized balls.
Place the balls on a plate and put in the
freezer for 10–12 minutes.

3. Meanwhile, place the candy melts in a
heatproof bowl set over a saucepan of gently
simmering water and heat until just melted.
Remove from the heat and stir until smooth.
Leave to cool for 5 minutes.

4. Remove the cake balls from the freezer.
Dip the end of a cake pop stick in the melted
candy and push into the centre of a cake
ball. Using a small palette knife, cover the
cake ball with melted candy, then sprinkle
liberally with sugar sprinkles. Stand in a tall
glass (see top tip, opposite) and place in the
refrigerator for a few minutes to set. Repeat
with the remaining cake balls, melted candy
and sprinkles.

makes 8

top tip

Fill the glass with dried beans or rice to stop the weight of the cake pops tipping the glass over.

cals: 254   fat: 11.3g   sat fat: 8.8g   fibre: 0.5g   carbs: 35.8g   sugar: 29.9g   salt: 0.2g   protein: 1.3g

blueberry cheesecake bars

prep: 30–35 mins, plus chilling and cooling
cook: 55–60 mins

200 g/7 oz digestive biscuits, crushed

70 g/2½ oz unsalted butter, melted, plus extra for greasing

175 g/6 oz blueberries

450 g/1 lb full-fat soft cheese

½ tsp vanilla extract

150 g/5½ oz caster sugar

3 eggs, beaten

150 ml/5 fl oz soured cream

1 tbsp cornflour

1. Preheat the oven to 150°C/300°F/Gas Mark 2. Grease a 28 x 18-cm/11 x 7-inch traybake tin and line with baking paper. Put the crushed biscuits into a bowl and stir in the melted butter. Press into the base of the prepared tin, levelling the surface with the back of a spoon. Chill in the refrigerator for 10–15 minutes.

2. Purée half the blueberries in a blender or food processor and set aside. Put the soft cheese, vanilla extract and sugar into a large bowl and beat with a wooden spoon until smooth. Gradually beat in the eggs, then fold in the soured cream and cornflour.

3. Scatter the remaining blueberries over the biscuit base, then spoon over the cheesecake mixture and gently level the surface with a spatula. Drop small spoonfuls of the reserved blueberry purée over the mixture, then drag the tip of a knife through the mixture to create a rippled effect.

4. Bake in the preheated oven for 50–55 minutes, or until just set. Turn off the oven and leave the cheesecake inside until cold, then transfer to the refrigerator and chill for 2–3 hours.

cals: 321   fat: 20.6g   sat fat: 11g   fibre: 1g   carbs: 28.3g   sugar: 18.7g   salt: 0.5g   protein: 5.5g

fluffy gingerbread cupcakes

prep: 45 mins, plus cooling and drying
cook: 20 mins

190 g/6¾ oz plain flour

1½ tsp baking powder

2 tsp ground ginger

1 tsp ground cinnamon

¼ tsp ground allspice

¼ tsp freshly grated nutmeg

¼ tsp salt

115 g/4 oz unsalted butter, softened

110 g/3¾ oz soft dark brown sugar

1 tsp vanilla extract

2 large eggs

160 g/5¾ oz treacle

125 ml/4 fl oz milk

frosting

175 g/6 oz cream cheese

55 g/2 oz unsalted butter, softened

500 g/1 lb 2 oz icing sugar, plus extra
   if needed

1 tsp ground ginger

finely grated rind of 1 lemon

2 tbsp lemon juice

pinch of salt

decoration

55 g/2 oz brown ready-to-roll fondant
   icing

white writing icing

1. Preheat the oven to 180°C/350°F/Gas Mark 4. Line a 12-hole muffin tin with 12 paper cases.

2. Sift together the flour, baking powder, ginger, cinnamon, allspice, nutmeg and salt into a bowl. Put the butter and brown sugar into a separate bowl and beat until pale and fluffy. Add the vanilla extract, then add the eggs, one at a time, beating well after each addition. Add half of the flour mixture, the treacle and milk and mix to incorporate. Fold in the remaining flour mixture.

3. Spoon the mixture into the paper cases. Bake in the preheated oven for 20 minutes, until risen and a cocktail stick inserted into the centre of a cupcake comes out clean. Leave to cool in the tin for 1–2 minutes, then transfer to a wire rack to cool completely.

4. To make the frosting, combine the cream cheese, butter, icing sugar, ginger, lemon rind, lemon juice and salt in a bowl and mix with a hand-held electric mixer until well combined. Add more icing sugar, if necessary, to achieve a piping consistency. Spoon the frosting into a piping bag fitted with a medium star-shaped nozzle and pipe onto the cupcakes.

5. To decorate, roll out the fondant icing until it is 5 mm/¼ inch thick. Cut out 12 mini gingerbread men shapes and set aside on a sheet of baking paper to dry.

6. Once hardened, use the white writing icing to pipe buttons and other decorations onto the gingerbread men shapes. To serve, place a gingerbread man on top of each cupcake.

top tip

For a simpler decoration, just scatter sugar sprinkles over the frosting.

makes 12

cals: 483   fat: 17g   sat fat: 10.1g   fibre: 0.7g   carbs: 85g   sugar: 71.6g   salt: 0.6g   protein: 4.5g

raisin flapjacks

prep: 15 mins, plus cooling
cook: 20-25 mins

140 g/5 oz rolled oats

115 g/4 oz demerara sugar

85 g/3 oz raisins

115 g/4 oz unsalted butter, melted,
plus extra for greasing

1. Preheat the oven to 190°C/375°F/Gas Mark 5. Grease a 28 x 18-cm/11 x 7-inch traybake tin.

2. Combine the oats, sugar and raisins with the butter in a mixing bowl, stirring well. Spoon the mixture into the prepared tin and press down firmly with the back of a spoon. Bake in the preheated oven for 15–20 minutes, or until golden.

3. Using a sharp knife, mark into 14 bars, then leave to cool in the tin for 10 minutes. Carefully transfer the bars to a wire rack to cool completely.

variation

You can use any type of dried fruit in place of the raisins – for a change, try chopped dried apricots, sultanas or dried cranberries.

cals: 152   fat: 8g   sat fat: 4.7g   fibre: 1.2g   carbs: 19.8g   sugar: 11.9g   salt: trace   protein: 1.6g

easy as pie

Take a glance in any patisserie shop window and you will see a tempting array of picture-perfect pastries and other melt-in-the-mouth confections. This chapter shows you how to whip up many of these classics – including croissants, macaroons, tuiles and florentines – in your own kitchen.

time saving

Whilst most of the recipes in this chapter involve making pastry from scratch, some use shop-bought pastry. This can be a useful cheat when you don't have the time or inclination to make your own, particularly in the case of puff pastry, which needs lengthy chilling and resting.

patisserie perfection

summer fruit tartlets — 82

vanilla macaroons — 84

croissants — 86

white chocolate-dipped madeleines — 88

raspberry & rosewater éclairs — 90

pistachio & almond tuiles — 92

powdered doughnuts — 94

morello cherry clafoutis — 96

tarte au citron — 98

CHOOSING INGREDIENTS — 100

cranberry & ginger florentines — 102

blueberry tarts — 104

pain au chocolat cinnamon rolls — 106

profiteroles — 108

caramelized apple tarts — 110

white chocolate passion éclairs — 112

cinnamon scones — 114

chocolate macaroon gateau — 116

summer fruit tartlets

prep: 35-40 mins, plus chilling and cooling
cook: 12-18 mins

200 g/7 oz plain flour, plus extra
   for dusting

85 g/3 oz icing sugar, plus extra
   for dusting

55 g/2 oz ground almonds

115 g/4 oz unsalted butter, diced

1 egg yolk

1 tbsp milk

filling

225 g/8 oz cream cheese

icing sugar, to taste

350 g/12 oz mixed berries, such
   as blueberries, strawberries and
   raspberries (halve or quarter the
   strawberries, if large)

1. Sift the flour and icing sugar into a bowl. Stir in the ground almonds. Rub in the butter with your fingertips until the mixture resembles breadcrumbs. Add the egg yolk and milk and mix to form a dough.

2. Wrap the dough in clingfilm and chill in the refrigerator for 30 minutes. Meanwhile, preheat the oven to 200°C/400°F/Gas Mark 6.

3. Roll out the dough on a lightly floured surface and use it to line 12 deep tartlet tins. Prick the bases and press a piece of aluminium foil into each. Bake in the preheated oven for 10–15 minutes, or until light golden. Remove the foil and bake for a further 2–3 minutes. Carefully transfer to a wire rack to cool completely.

4. Place the cream cheese and icing sugar in a bowl and mix together. Place a spoonful of filling in each tartlet and arrange the berries on top. Dust with icing sugar.

3

variation

Mixed berries work well in these tempting tartlets, but a single berry — such as strawberries — would be equally delicious.

makes 12

cals: 254   fat: 14.8g   sat fat: 8g   fibre: 1.9g   carbs: 25.8g   sugar: 11.8g   salt: 0.2g   protein: 4.5g

vanilla macaroons

prep: 40 mins, plus standing and cooling
cook: 10-15 mins

75 g/2¾ oz ground almonds
115 g/4 oz icing sugar
2 large egg whites
50 g/1¾ oz caster sugar
½ tsp vanilla extract

filling
55 g/2 oz unsalted butter, softened
½ tsp vanilla extract
115 g/4 oz icing sugar, sifted

variation

For chocolate-flavoured macaroon shells, replace 15 g/½ oz of the icing sugar with 2 tablespoons of cocoa powder and omit the vanilla extract.

1. Place the ground almonds and icing sugar in a food processor and process for 15 seconds. Sift the mixture into a bowl. Line two baking sheets with baking paper.

2. Place the egg whites in a large bowl and whisk until holding soft peaks. Gradually whisk in the caster sugar to make a firm, glossy meringue. Whisk in the vanilla extract.

3. Using a spatula, fold the almond mixture into the meringue one third at a time. When all the dry ingredients are thoroughly incorporated, continue to cut and fold the mixture until it forms a shiny batter with a thick, ribbon-like consistency.

4. Spoon the mixture into a piping bag fitted with a 1-cm/½-inch plain nozzle. Pipe 32 small rounds onto the prepared baking sheets. Tap the baking sheets firmly onto a work surface to remove any air bubbles. Leave at room temperature for 30 minutes. Preheat the oven to 160°C/325°F/Gas Mark 3.

5. Bake the macaroons in the preheated oven for 10–15 minutes. Leave to cool for 10 minutes, then carefully transfer the macaroons to a wire rack to cool completely.

6. To make the filling, beat the butter and vanilla extract in a bowl until pale and fluffy. Gradually beat in the icing sugar until smooth and creamy. Use to sandwich pairs of macaroons together.

croissants

prep: 45-55 mins, plus rising and chilling
cook: 20-25 mins

500 g/1 lb 2 oz strong white flour,
plus extra for dusting

40 g/1½ oz caster sugar

1 tsp salt

2¼ tsp easy-blend dried yeast

300 ml/10 fl oz lukewarm milk,
plus extra if needed

300 g/10½ oz unsalted butter, softened,
plus extra for greasing

1 egg, lightly beaten with 1 tbsp milk,
for glazing

1. Stir the dry ingredients in a large bowl, make a well in the centre and add the milk. Mix to form a soft dough, adding more milk if too dry. Knead on a lightly floured work surface for 5–10 minutes, or until smooth and elastic. Place in a large, greased bowl, cover with clingfilm and leave to rise in a warm place until doubled in size. Meanwhile, put the butter between two sheets of greaseproof paper and use a rolling pin to flatten to form a rectangle about 5 mm/¼ inch thick. Chill in the refrigerator.

2. Preheat the oven to 200°C/400°F/Gas Mark 6. Knead the dough for 1 minute. Remove the butter from the refrigerator and leave to soften slightly.

3. Roll out the dough on a well-floured work surface to form a rectangle measuring 46 x 15 cm/18 x 6 inches. Place the butter in the centre, fold up the sides and squeeze the edges together gently. With the short end of the dough towards you, fold the top third down towards the centre, then fold the bottom third up. Rotate 90 degrees clockwise so that the fold is to your left and the top flap opens towards your right. Roll out to a rectangle and fold again. If the butter feels soft, wrap the dough in clingfilm and chill. Repeat the rolling process twice more.

4. Cut the dough in half. Roll out one half into a 5 mm/¼ inch thick triangle (keep the other half refrigerated). Use a triangular card template with a base of 18 cm/7 inches and sides of 20 cm/8 inches to cut out six croissants. Repeat with the refrigerated dough.

5. Brush the triangles lightly with the egg glaze. Roll into croissant shapes, starting at the base and tucking the point under to prevent them from unrolling while cooking. Brush again with the glaze. Place on an ungreased baking sheet and leave to double in size. Bake in the preheated oven for 15–20 minutes, or until golden brown.

makes 12

top tip

Making your own croissants requires time and patience but it's worth it for the results.

cals: 374   fat: 22.9g   sat fat: 14g   fibre: 1.2g   carbs: 34.1g   sugar: 5.1g   salt: 0.5g   protein: 8.3g

white chocolate-dipped madeleines

prep: 25-30 mins, plus standing and cooling
cook: 18-20 mins

2 eggs

50 g/1¾ oz soft light brown sugar

50 g/1¾ oz caster sugar

100 g/3½ oz plain flour, sifted,
plus extra for dusting

100 g/3½ oz unsalted butter, melted,
plus extra for greasing

1 tsp baking powder

½ tsp ground cinnamon

2 tbsp cocoa powder, sifted

1 tsp vanilla extract

100 g/3½ oz white chocolate, broken
into pieces

1. Preheat the oven to 200°C/400°F/Gas Mark 6. Lightly grease a 12-hole madeleine tin and dust with flour.

2. Place the eggs, brown sugar and caster sugar in a mixing bowl and beat well until the mixture is light and frothy.

3. Lightly fold in the flour, melted butter, baking powder, cinnamon, cocoa powder and vanilla extract. Leave to stand for 20 minutes.

4. Divide the mixture between the holes in the prepared tin. Bake in the preheated oven for 8–10 minutes, until well risen. Leave to cool in the tin for 1–2 minutes, then transfer to a wire rack to cool completely.

5. Place the chocolate in a heatproof bowl set over a saucepan of gently simmering water and heat until melted. Dip one end of each madeleine in the melted chocolate and leave to set on a baking sheet.

top tip

These tempting morsels are best eaten on the day of making. Dipping them in melted chocolate is optional but it tastes good!

raspberry & rosewater éclairs

prep: 55 mins, plus cooling and setting
cook: 30 mins

choux pastry
50 g/1¾ oz unsalted butter
150 ml/5 fl oz cold water
70 g/2½ oz plain flour, sifted
pinch of salt
2 eggs, beaten

filling
300 ml/10 fl oz double cream
1 tsp rosewater
200 g/7 oz small raspberries

icing
200 g/7 oz icing sugar
½ tsp rosewater
1½–2 tbsp lukewarm water
a few drops of pink food colouring

1. Preheat the oven to 220°C/425°F/ Gas Mark 7. Line a large baking sheet with baking paper.

2. To make the pastry, put the butter and water into a saucepan and heat gently until the butter has melted. Bring to a rolling boil, remove from the heat and quickly beat in the flour and salt until the mixture forms a ball that leaves the sides of the pan clean. Transfer to a bowl and leave to cool for 5 minutes.

3. Gradually beat in the eggs to form a smooth, glossy mixture with a soft, dropping consistency. Spoon into a piping bag fitted with a 15-mm/⅝-inch plain nozzle and pipe 12 éclairs, each about 12 cm/4½ inches long, onto the prepared baking sheet. Sprinkle a little water around the éclairs.

4. Bake in the preheated oven for 20 minutes, or until golden. Remove from the oven and use the tip of a knife to pierce a hole in each éclair. Return to the oven for a further 5 minutes. Transfer the éclairs to a wire rack to cool completely.

5. Put the cream into a bowl with the rosewater and whip until it holds soft peaks. For the icing, sift the icing sugar into a separate bowl and stir in the rosewater and enough of the water to make a thick, spreadable icing. Remove 2 tablespoons of the icing and add enough food colouring to tint it a deep pink. Spoon the pink icing into a paper piping bag and snip off the end.

6. To assemble, split the éclairs lengthways and fill with small spoonfuls of the whipped cream and the raspberries. Gently spread the white icing over the tops of the éclairs. Whilst the white icing is still wet, pipe three lines of pink icing along the length of each éclair, then drag a cocktail stick backwards and forwards through the icing to create a feathered effect. Leave to set.

top tip

Fill and ice a few éclairs at a time, otherwise the icing will set before you have a chance to create the feathered effect.

makes 12

cals: 247   fat: 16.3g   sat fat: 9.9g   fibre: 1.2g   carbs: 23.5g   sugar: 17.8g   salt: 0.3g   protein: 2.4g

pistachio & almond tuiles

prep: 25-30 mins, plus setting and cooling
cook: 12-18 mins

1 egg white

55 g/2 oz golden caster sugar

25 g/1 oz plain flour

25 g/1 oz pistachio nuts,
  finely chopped

25 g/1 oz ground almonds

½ tsp almond extract

40 g/1½ oz unsalted butter,
  melted and cooled

1. Preheat the oven to 160°C/325°F/
Gas Mark 3. Line two baking sheets with
baking paper.

2. Whisk the egg white lightly with the sugar,
then stir in the flour, pistachio nuts, ground
almonds, almond extract and butter, mixing to
form a soft paste.

3. Place walnut-sized spoonfuls of the mixture
on the prepared baking sheets and use the
back of the spoon to spread as thinly as
possible. Bake in the preheated oven for
10–15 minutes, until pale golden.

4. Quickly lift each biscuit with a palette knife
and place over the side of a rolling pin while
still warm to shape into a curve. When set,
transfer to a wire rack to cool completely.

top tip

The tuiles need to be warm when you shape
them. If they cool down too much to shape,
return them to the oven for a minute or so.

cals: 150   fat: 9.5g   sat fat: 3.8g   fibre: 1g   carbs: 14.3g   sugar: 9.7g   salt: trace   protein: 2.8g

powdered doughnuts

prep: 25–30 mins, plus chilling and cooling
cook: 14–17 mins

250 g/9 oz self-raising flour,
   plus extra if needed and for dusting

1½ tsp baking powder

½ tsp ground mixed spice

¼ tsp salt

55 g/2 oz caster sugar

1 large egg, beaten

100 ml/3½ fl oz milk

25 g/1 oz unsalted butter, melted and
   slightly cooled

½ tsp vanilla extract

vegetable oil, for deep-frying

115 g/4 oz icing sugar

top tip

Only toss the doughnuts in the icing sugar just before serving because the sugar will dissolve into the warm doughnuts. If this happens, simply dust with more icing sugar.

1. Sift together the flour, baking powder and mixed spice into a large bowl. Stir in the salt and caster sugar. Make a well in the centre.

2. Put the egg, milk, melted butter and vanilla extract into a jug, mix together and pour into the well. Mix to a medium-soft dough, adding a little extra flour if the dough is too sticky to handle. Cover and chill in the refrigerator for 30 minutes.

3. Roll out the dough on a lightly floured surface to a thickness of 15 mm/⅝ inch. Use a 7.5-cm/3-inch doughnut cutter to stamp out eight doughnuts

4. Heat enough oil for deep-frying in a large saucepan or deep-fryer to 180–190°C/350–375°F, or until a cube of bread browns in 30 seconds. Add the doughnuts, a few at a time, and fry, turning frequently, for 3–4 minutes, or until crisp and deep golden. Remove and drain on kitchen paper. Leave to cool for 10 minutes.

5. Sift the icing sugar into a shallow bowl and toss the doughnuts in it to coat thoroughly. Serve immediately.

makes 8

cals: 301   fat: 10.8g   sat fat: 2.8g   fibre: 0.9g   carbs: 46.1g   sugar: 22g   salt: 1.5g   protein: 4.6g

morello cherry clafoutis

prep: 25-30 mins, plus resting
cook: 22 mins

2 eggs, separated
60 g/2¼ oz caster sugar
1 tbsp vanilla sugar
100 g/3½ oz plain flour
200 ml/7 fl oz milk
pinch of salt
pinch of grated lemon rind
250 g/9 oz morello cherries
2 tbsp vegetable oil
icing sugar, for dusting
whipped cream, to serve (optional)

1. Put the egg yolks, caster sugar and vanilla sugar into a large bowl and beat with a hand-held electric mixer until fluffy. Add the flour, milk, salt and lemon rind and beat until smooth. Leave to rest for 30 minutes.

2. Preheat the oven to 180°C/350°F/Gas Mark 4. Stone the cherries.

3. Whisk the egg whites until they hold stiff peaks, then carefully fold them into the batter.

4. Heat the oil in a 28-cm/11-inch ovenproof frying pan. Pour in the batter and cook over a low heat for 5 minutes, until the underside is lightly browned. Scatter the cherries over the surface.

5. Transfer the pan to the preheated oven and bake for about 15 minutes. Slide the clafoutis out of the pan onto a cake plate. Dust with icing sugar and serve warm with whipped cream, if using.

cals: 165   fat: 5.7g   sat fat: 1.3g   fibre: 0.8g   carbs: 24.6g   sugar: 14g   salt: 0.4g   protein: 4.1g

tarte au citron

prep: 30 mins, plus chilling and cooling
cook: 30 mins

pastry

3 tbsp water

1 tbsp caster sugar

pinch of salt

1 tbsp vegetable oil

90 g/3¼ oz unsalted butter, diced

150 g/5½ oz plain flour, plus extra
for dusting

filling

2 eggs

2 egg yolks

125 ml/4 fl oz freshly squeezed
lemon juice

grated rind of 1 lemon

100 g/3½ oz caster sugar

85 g/3 oz unsalted butter, diced

1. Preheat the oven to 200°C/400°F/Gas Mark 6. To make the pastry, mix together the water, sugar, salt, oil and butter with the flour. Chill in the refrigerator for 20 minutes.

2. Roll out the dough on a lightly floured surface to a thickness of 5 mm/¼ inch. Use to line a 23-cm/9-inch round tart tin, trimming the edges. Prick the base all over with a fork. Bake in the preheated oven for 15 minutes, until golden brown. Remove from the oven and leave to cool in the tin. Do not switch off the oven.

3. Meanwhile, beat together the eggs and egg yolks and set aside.

4. Put the lemon juice, lemon rind, sugar and butter into a saucepan over a medium heat and heat until the butter has melted. Reduce the heat, add the beaten egg and cook, stirring constantly, until the mixture has thickened and bubbles are beginning to form.

5. Pour the lemon and egg mixture through a sieve into the pastry case, evenly spreading the mixture with the back of a spoon. Return to the oven for 5 minutes. Remove from the oven and leave to cool. Serve cold.

top tip

To avoid spillage, put the tart tin in the oven before pouring in the lemon filling in step 5.

serves 8

cals: 338   fat: 22.1g   sat fat: 12.3g   fibre: 0.7g   carbs: 31.1g   sugar: 14.9g   salt: 0.4g   protein: 4.8g

choosing ingredients

Whatever you choose to bake, the finest quality ingredients will always give the best flavour. Here's a guide to some of the ingredients you're likely to need.

the essentials

Flour

• White flour is the most refined type of flour milled from soft wheat grains. Self-raising flour has added baking powder.

• Wholemeal and wholewheat flours are milled from the entire wheat grain and impart a lovely nutty flavour. They have a coarser texture than white flours and will absorb more liquid.

• Bread or strong flours are milled from hard wheat, which has a high gluten content, making them perfect for bread making.

• Cornflour is a fine white powder made from maize. Often used as a thickening agent, it can also be added to cake, shortbread and cookies to give a light and crisp texture.

Fats

• Butter has a wonderful rich flavour. Use unsalted butter for frostings and delicately flavoured cakes.
• Margarine can be used in place of butter but won't give the same buttery taste. Low-fat margarines and spreads are not suitable for baking.
• Lard is a hard animal fat traditionally used in pastry making. White vegetable fat is a healthier alternative that is suitable for vegetarians.
• Oil is sometimes used in cake making and will produce a moist cake. Use mild flavoured oils, such as sunflower.

Sugars and syrups

• With its fine grains, caster sugar is ideal for baking. Unrefined golden caster sugar has a pale golden colour and a light caramel flavour.
• Soft light and dark brown sugars have more depth of flavour than white sugars and add richness and colour to your baking.
• Demerara sugar has large, golden crystals that add crunch and texture to crumble toppings or when sprinkled over cakes and cookies.
• Icing sugar has a fine, powdery texture that dissolves easily, making it essential for icings and frostings.
• Golden syrup, black treacle, honey and maple syrup are all useful sweet syrups. They can be used in place of sugar in some recipes.

Eggs

• For best results, always use eggs at room temperature. Make sure that you have the correct size for the recipe – unless otherwise stated, the recipes in this book use medium-sized eggs.

Raising agents

• Baking powder, bicarbonate of soda, cream of tartar and dried yeast are all raising agents. They have a limited shelf life so make sure to check their 'best before' date before using and always store in a cool, dry place.

Flavourings

• Vanilla, almond and other flavouring extracts can give a flavour boost to your baked goods. Try to buy natural extracts rather than synthetic flavourings.

Dried fruits and nuts

• Dried fruits keep well stored in sealed bags or airtight containers. Glacé fruits, such as cherries, should be rinsed and dried before use to remove their syrupy coating.
• Chopped nuts give flavour and texture to cakes and cookies, and ground nuts add extra moistness. Because of their high oil content, nuts can go rancid quickly so buy them in small quantities and store in a cool, dark place. Where possible, buy whole nuts and chop or grind them just before using.

Chocolate

• When buying plain chocolate, choose one that contains between 50 to 70 per cent cocoa solids. Milk, plain or white chocolate chips or chocolate chunks make a tasty addition to cookies, muffins and cupcakes.

cranberry & ginger florentines

prep: 35 mins, plus cooling and setting
cook: 20–22 mins

70 g/2½ oz light muscovado sugar

55 g/2 oz runny honey

100 g/3½ oz unsalted butter, plus extra
for greasing

50 g /1¾ oz desiccated coconut

70 g/2½ oz flaked almonds

1 tbsp finely chopped candied peel

1 tbsp finely chopped crystallized
stem ginger

100 g/3½ oz dried cranberries

50 g/1¾ oz plain flour, plus extra
for dusting

250 g/9 oz plain chocolate,
roughly chopped

top tip

These crispy, chewy bites make a marvellous present — simply pack them into a clear cellophane bag and tie with a pretty ribbon.

1. Preheat the oven to 180°C/350°F/Gas Mark 4. Lightly grease four 12-hole mini muffin tins (the base of each hole should be 2 cm/¾ inch in diameter), then lightly dust them with flour.

2. Put the muscovado sugar, honey and butter into a heavy-based saucepan. Heat gently, stirring, until the sugar has dissolved, tilting the pan to mix the ingredients together. Stir in the desiccated coconut, flaked almonds, candied peel, crystallized ginger, dried cranberries and flour.

3. Put small teaspoonfuls of the mixture into the prepared muffin tins. Bake in the preheated oven for 10–12 minutes, or until golden brown. Leave to cool in the tins for 1 hour. Using a palette knife, transfer to a wire rack to firm up.

4. Put the chocolate in a heatproof bowl set over a saucepan of gently simmering water and heat until melted. Leave to cool slightly. Dip each florentine into the melted chocolate so the base is covered. Place on a wire rack, chocolate side up, and leave to set.

cals: 84   fat: 5.4g   sat fat: 3g   fibre: 0.9g   carbs: 8.6g   sugar: 6.1g   salt: trace   protein: 0.8g

blueberry tarts

prep: 35 mins, plus cooling
cook: 17–18 mins

300 g/10½ oz blueberries

2 tsp cornflour

55 g/2 oz caster sugar

4 tsp water

55 g/2 oz plain flour,
   plus extra for dusting

grated rind of 1 lemon

40 g/1½ oz unsalted butter, diced,
   plus extra for greasing

325 g/11½ oz ready-made sweet
   shortcrust pastry, chilled

1. Preheat the oven to 190°C/375°F/Gas Mark 5. Lightly grease two 12-hole mini muffin tins.

2. Put half the blueberries in a small saucepan with the cornflour, half the caster sugar and the water. Cook, uncovered, over a medium heat, stirring constantly, for 2–3 minutes, or until the juices begin to run and the sauce thickens. Take the pan off the heat and add the remaining blueberries.

3. To make the streusel topping, put the flour, lemon rind and the remaining sugar in a mixing bowl. Rub in the butter with your fingertips until the mixture resembles fine breadcrumbs. Set aside.

4. Roll out the pastry thinly on a lightly floured surface. Using a 6-cm/2½-inch fluted round cutter, stamp out 24 circles. Press these into the prepared tins. Spoon the blueberry filling into the cases, then sprinkle the tops of the tarts with the streusel mixture.

5. Bake in the preheated oven for 15 minutes, or until the topping is light golden. Leave to cool in the tins for 10 minutes, then loosen with a round-bladed knife and transfer to a wire rack to cool. Serve warm or cold.

top tip

Sweet shortcrust pastry is useful for making desserts and tarts. It's available from most supermarkets.

makes 24

cals: 96   fat: 4.3g   sat fat: 2.4g   fibre: 0.8g   carbs: 13.4g   sugar: 5.7g   salt: trace   protein: 1.1g

pain au chocolat cinnamon rolls

prep: 30 mins, plus cooling and chilling
cook: 20–25 mins

100 g/3½ oz plain chocolate,
   broken into pieces
320 g/11 oz ready-rolled puff pastry
25 g/1 oz unsalted butter, melted
2 tbsp caster sugar
1½ tsp ground cinnamon
icing sugar, for dusting (optional)

1. Put the chocolate into a heatproof bowl set over a saucepan of gently simmering water and heat until melted. Stir until smooth, then leave to cool for 15 minutes.

2. Generously brush the pastry sheet with some of the melted butter. Leave to cool for 10 minutes, then spread the cooled chocolate all over the buttered pastry. Combine the sugar and cinnamon in a bowl, then sprinkle over the chocolate.

3. Roll up the pastry, Swiss roll-style, from one long side, then brush all over with more of the melted butter. Chill in the refrigerator for 15 minutes. Meanwhile, preheat the oven to 220°C/425°F/Gas Mark 7. Use the remaining melted butter to grease a 12-hole muffin tin.

4. Using a serrated knife, slice the pastry roll into 12 equal-sized rounds. Place each round, cut-side up, in a hole in the prepared tin.

5. Bake in the preheated oven for 15–20 minutes, or until risen and golden brown. Leave to cool in the tin for 5 minutes, then transfer to a wire rack. Dust with icing sugar, if using, and serve warm or cold.

variation

For a mocha filling, replace the cinnamon with 2 teaspoons finely ground coffee granules.

cals: 175   fat: 11.3g   sat fat: 6.2g   fibre: 1.4g   carbs: 16.5g   sugar: 5.9g   salt: 0.2g   protein: 1.8g

profiteroles

prep: 35-40 mins, plus cooling
cook: 35 mins

choux pastry

70 g/2½ oz unsalted butter,
   plus extra for greasing
200 ml/7 fl oz water
100 g/3½ oz plain flour
3 eggs, beaten

cream filling

300 ml/10 fl oz double cream
3 tbsp caster sugar
1 tsp vanilla extract

chocolate sauce

125 g/4½ oz plain chocolate, broken
   into pieces
35 g/1¼ oz unsalted butter
6 tbsp water
2 tbsp brandy

top tip

Piercing the choux pastry balls immediately after they come out of the oven allows the steam to escape and keeps the outsides crisp; the insides should be slightly sticky.

1. Preheat the oven to 200°C/400°F/Gas Mark 6. Grease several large baking sheets.

2. To make the pastry, place the butter and water in a saucepan and bring to the boil. Meanwhile, sift the flour into a bowl. Turn off the heat and beat in the flour until smooth. Leave to cool for 5 minutes. Beat in enough of the eggs to give the mixture a soft, dropping consistency.

3. Transfer to a piping bag fitted with a 1-cm/½-inch plain nozzle. Pipe small balls onto the prepared baking sheets. Bake in the preheated oven for 25 minutes. Remove from the oven. Pierce each ball with a skewer to let the steam escape.

4. To make the filling, whip the cream, sugar and vanilla extract until holding soft peaks. Cut the pastry balls across the middle, then fill with the cream.

5. To make the sauce, gently melt the chocolate, butter and water together in a small saucepan, stirring constantly, until smooth. Stir in the brandy.

6. Pile the profiteroles into individual serving dishes and pour over the sauce.

cals: 931   fat: 75.2g   sat fat: 45.3g   fibre: 3.2g   carbs: 48.3g   sugar: 24.2g   salt: 0.1g   protein: 11.1g

caramelized apple tarts

prep: 45 mins, plus chilling and cooling
cook: 37-43 mins

450 g/1 lb ready-made sweet
  shortcrust pastry, chilled

plain flour, for dusting

5 Granny Smith apples, peeled, cored
  and quartered

85 g/3 oz caster sugar

juice and finely grated rind of 1 lemon

2 eggs

15 g/½ oz unsalted butter, plus extra
  for greasing

3 tbsp icing sugar, sifted

top tip

Baking the pastry cases before adding
a wet filling, like the apples, helps to
keep them crisp and prevents them from
developing soggy bottoms.

1. Lightly grease a 12-hole muffin tin. Roll out the pastry thinly on a lightly floured surface. Using a 10-cm/4-inch plain round cutter, stamp out 12 circles. Press these gently into the prepared tin. Prick the base of each with a fork, then chill in the refrigerator for 15 minutes. Preheat the oven to 190°C/375°F/Gas Mark 5.

2. Line the pastry cases with squares of baking paper and baking beans. Bake in the preheated oven for 10 minutes. Remove the paper and beans and cook the cases for a further 2–3 minutes, or until the base of the pastry is crisp and dry. Reduce the oven temperature to 180°C/350°F/Gas Mark 4.

3. Roughly grate eight of the apple quarters into a mixing bowl. Add 55 g/2 oz of the caster sugar, the lemon juice, lemon rind and the eggs and whisk together. Spoon the filling into the pastry cases.

4. Thinly slice the remaining apples and arrange them, overlapping, on top of the tarts. Sprinkle the tops with the remaining caster sugar, then dot the tarts with the butter. Bake in the preheated oven for 20–25 minutes, or until the filling is set.

5. Dust with the icing sugar and return the pies to the oven for 5 minutes, or until the sugar has caramelized. Leave to cool in the tin for 10 minutes, then transfer the tarts to a wire rack to cool. Serve warm or cold.

cals: 254   fat: 9.7g   sat fat: 4.9g   fibre: 2g   carbs: 39.3g   sugar: 23.6g   salt: trace   protein: 3.6g

white chocolate
passion éclairs

prep: 50-55 mins, plus cooling and setting
cook: 35 mins

choux pastry

50 g/1¾ oz unsalted butter
150 ml/5 fl oz cold water
60 g/2¼ oz plain flour, sifted
pinch of salt
2 large eggs, beaten

filling

200 ml/7 fl oz double cream
2 passion fruit

topping

200 g/7 oz white chocolate,
   broken into pieces
yellow writing icing

1. Preheat the oven to 200°C/400°F/Gas
Mark 6. Line two baking sheets with baking
paper.

2. Place the butter and water in a medium-
sized saucepan and bring to the boil. Add the
flour and salt and beat well until the mixture
starts to come away from the sides of the
pan. Remove from the heat and leave to cool
for 1–2 minutes.

3. Gradually beat in the eggs until the mixture
is smooth and glossy. Transfer to a piping
bag fitted with a 2.5-cm/1-inch plain nozzle
and pipe ten 8-cm/3¼-inch éclairs onto the
prepared baking sheets.

4. Bake in the preheated oven for 15 minutes,
then remove from the oven and use a fine
skewer to make a slit along the length of each
éclair to allow the steam to escape. Return to
the oven and bake for a further 10 minutes,
then transfer to a wire rack to cool.

5. Whip the cream until it just holds stiff
peaks. Cut the passion fruit in half and use
a teaspoon to remove the flesh. Stir into
the cream and use either a piping bag or a
teaspoon to fill the éclairs with the mixture.

6. To make the topping, place the chocolate in a heatproof bowl set over a saucepan of gently simmering water and heat until melted. Use a teaspoon to spread the melted chocolate evenly over the top of the éclairs.

7. Whilst the chocolate is still wet, pipe two or three lines of yellow writing icing along the length of each éclair, then drag a cocktail stick backwards and forwards through the icing to create a feathered effect. Leave to set.

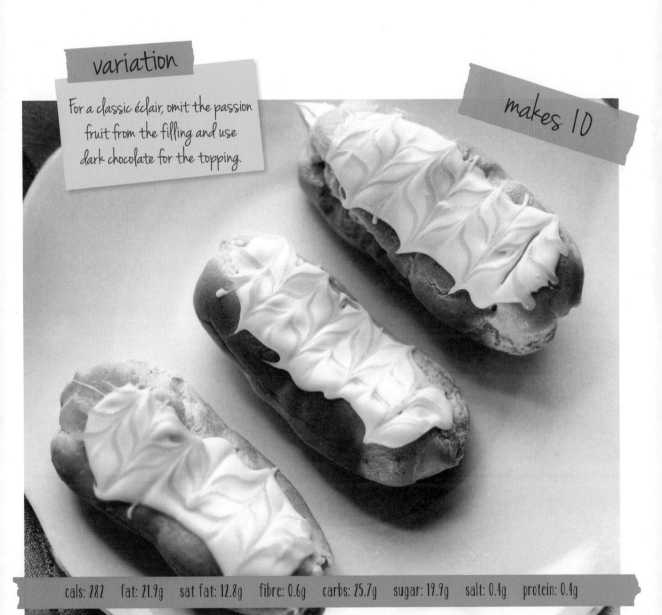

variation

For a classic éclair, omit the passion fruit from the filling and use dark chocolate for the topping.

makes 10

cals: 282   fat: 21.9g   sat fat: 12.8g   fibre: 0.6g   carbs: 25.7g   sugar: 19.9g   salt: 0.4g   protein: 0.4g

cinnamon scones

prep: 30 mins, plus cooling and setting
cook: 12-15 mins

250 g/9 oz self-raising flour,
  plus extra for dusting

1½ tsp baking powder

pinch of salt

1 tsp ground cinnamon

55 g/2 oz chilled unsalted butter,
  diced, plus extra for greasing and
  to serve (optional)

40 g/1½ oz caster sugar

55 g/2 oz sultanas

150 ml/5 fl oz milk, plus extra
  for glazing

icing

55 g/2 oz icing sugar

½ tsp ground cinnamon

1–2 tbsp lukewarm water

top tip

Make a tangy orange butter to spread on the split scones by beating grated orange rind into softened unsalted butter.

1. Preheat the oven to 220°C/425°F/Gas Mark 7. Lightly grease a large baking sheet and dust with flour.

2. Sift the flour, baking powder, salt and cinnamon into a large bowl. Rub in the butter with your fingertips until the mixture resembles fine breadcrumbs. Stir in the caster sugar and sultanas. Pour in the milk and mix to form a soft dough.

3. Turn out onto a floured work surface and knead lightly until smooth. Roll out to a thickness of 2 cm/¾ inch. Using a 7-cm/2¾-inch plain round cutter, stamp out eight rounds, re-rolling the dough as necessary.

4. Place the scones on the prepared baking sheet and brush with milk to glaze. Bake in the preheated oven for 12–15 minutes, or until risen and golden. Transfer to a wire rack to cool.

5. To make the icing, sift together the icing sugar and cinnamon into a bowl and stir in enough of the water to make a smooth icing. Drizzle over the scones and leave to set. Serve with butter, if using.

cals: 252   fat: 7.6g   sat fat: 4.6g   fibre: 1.4g   carbs: 42g   sugar: 17.1g   salt: 1.7g   protein: 4.1g

chocolate macaroon gateau

prep: 40 mins, plus cooling
cook: 30-35 mins

85 g/3 oz plain chocolate, broken
   into pieces

175 g/6 oz unsalted butter, softened,
   plus extra for greasing

175 g/6 oz caster sugar

175 g/6 oz self-raising flour

½ tsp baking powder

3 large eggs, beaten

2 tbsp cocoa powder

14 chocolate macaroon shells
   (see variation on page 84)

50 g/1¾ oz white and plain chocolate
   curls, to decorate

icing

175 g/6 oz plain chocolate,
   finely chopped

450 ml/15 fl oz double cream

1. Preheat the oven to 180°C/350°F/Gas
Mark 4. Grease two 23-cm/9-inch sandwich
tins and line the bases with baking paper.

2. Melt the chocolate in a heatproof bowl
set over a pan of gently simmering water.
Remove from the heat and leave to cool,
stirring occasionally.

3. Place the butter, sugar, flour, baking powder,
eggs and cocoa in a large bowl and, using a
hand-held electric mixer, beat until smooth
and creamy. Fold in the melted chocolate.

4. Spoon the mixture into the prepared tins
and level the surfaces. Bake in the preheated
oven for 20–25 minutes, or until risen and
just firm to the touch. Leave to cool in the
tins for 5 minutes, then turn out onto a wire
rack to cool completely.

5. For the icing, place the chocolate in a
heatproof bowl. Heat 300 ml/10 fl oz of the
cream in a saucepan until just boiling, then
pour over the chocolate and stir until smooth.
Leave to cool for 20–30 minutes, stirring
occasionally, until thick enough to spread.
Whip the remaining cream until holding
soft peaks.

6. Sandwich the cakes together with one third
of the chocolate icing and all the whipped
cream. Spread the remaining icing over
the top and sides of the cake. Gently press
the macaroon shells onto the icing around
the side of the cake. Decorate the top with
chocolate curls.

cals: 502   fat: 36.2g   sat fat: 21.4g   fibre: 2.5g   carbs: 39.7g   sugar: 26.4g   salt: 0.5g   protein: 5.7g

the slice is right

A wickedly indulgent dessert is a great way to round off a special meal, but this chapter also features many lighter, fruit-based options that can be enjoyed on a more regular basis. From fruit pies and crumbles to tempting cheesecakes and tarts, you're sure to find your perfect pudding.

decadent desserts

apple pie → 120
mocha puddings → 122
new york cheesecake → 124
tarte tatin → 126
cappuccino soufflés → 128
pumpkin pies → 130
apple & blackberry crumble → 132
banoffee meringue pie → 134
plum & almond filo tart → 136
BAKING SECRETS → 138
chocolate bread & butter pudding → 140
peach cobbler → 142
baked lemon cheesecake → 144
spiced pear & sultana strudel → 146
black-bottom pecan pie → 148
blood orange polenta tart → 150
zebra puddings → 152

apple pie

prep: 35-40 mins, plus chilling
cook: 50 mins

pastry

350 g/12 oz plain flour, plus extra
for dusting

pinch of salt

85 g/3 oz butter or margarine, diced

85 g/3 oz lard or white vegetable
fat, diced

6 tbsp cold water

milk, for glazing

filling

900 g/2 lb cooking apples, peeled, cored
and sliced

125 g/4½ oz caster sugar, plus extra
for sprinkling

½–1 tsp ground cinnamon, ground
mixed spice or ground ginger

1. To make the pastry, sift the flour and salt into a mixing bowl. Add the butter and lard and rub in with your fingertips until the mixture resembles fine breadcrumbs. Add the water and gather the mixture together into a dough.

2. Wrap the dough in clingfilm and chill in the refrigerator for 30 minutes.

3. Preheat the oven to 220°C/425°F/Gas Mark 7. Roll out almost two thirds of the pastry thinly on a lightly floured surface and use to line a deep 23-cm/9-inch pie dish.

4. To make the filling, place the apple slices, sugar and spice in a bowl and mix together thoroughly. Pack the apple mixture into the pastry case; the filling can come up above the rim. Add 1–2 tablespoons of water if needed.

5. Roll out the remaining pastry on a lightly floured surface to form a lid. Dampen the edges of the pie rim with water and position the lid, pressing the edges firmly together. Trim and crimp the edges. Use the trimmings to cut out leaves or other shapes to decorate the top of the pie. Dampen and attach. Glaze the top of the pie with milk, make a slit in the top and place the pie dish on a baking sheet.

6. Bake in the preheated oven for 20 minutes, then reduce the temperature to 180°C/350°F/ Gas Mark 4 and bake for a further 30 minutes, or until the pastry is a light golden brown. Serve hot or cold, sprinkled with sugar.

serves 8

top tip

To prevent the apple slices from discolouring, put them in a bowl of water with the juice of a lemon.

cals: 453   fat: 20g   sat fat: 9.8g   fibre: 2.9g   carbs: 64.8g   sugar: 27.3g   salt: 0.6g   protein: 5.2g

mocha puddings

prep: 25 mins
cook: 20-25 mins

175 g/6 oz plain flour

2 tbsp cocoa powder

2 tsp baking powder

175 g/6 oz unsalted butter, softened, plus extra for greasing

175 g/6 oz light muscovado sugar

3 eggs, beaten

1 tsp coffee extract

30 g/1 oz plain chocolate, broken into 6 small squares

sauce

250 ml/9 fl oz single cream

100 g/3½ oz plain chocolate, broken into pieces

1 tsp coffee extract

variation

Adding coffee extract to these tempting little puddings gives them a rich depth of flavour. However, if you're not a fan of coffee, simply leave it out

1. Preheat the oven to 200°C/400°F/Gas Mark 6. Grease six 200-ml/7-fl oz metal pudding basins.

2. Sift the flour, cocoa and baking powder into a large bowl and add the butter, sugar, eggs and coffee extract. Beat well until smooth.

3. Spoon the mixture into the prepared pudding basins. Place a square of chocolate on top of each. Bake in the preheated oven for 20–25 minutes, or until risen and firm to the touch.

4. Meanwhile, make the sauce. Place the cream, chocolate and coffee extract in a small saucepan and heat gently without boiling, stirring, until melted and smooth. Turn out the puddings and serve with the sauce poured over them.

new york cheesecake

prep: 35 mins, plus cooling and chilling
cook: 1 hour

100 g/3½ oz unsalted butter, plus extra
  for greasing
150 g/5½ oz digestive biscuits,
  finely crushed
1 tbsp granulated sugar
900 g/2 lb cream cheese
250 g/9 oz caster sugar
2 tbsp plain flour
1 tsp vanilla extract
finely grated rind of 1 orange
finely grated rind of 1 lemon
3 eggs
2 egg yolks
300 ml/10 fl oz double cream

top tip

It's important to leave the cheesecake in the switched-off oven in step 4 as it will continue to cook as it cools. It should be softly set with a slight wobble.

1. Preheat the oven to 180°C/350°F/Gas Mark 4.

2. Melt the butter in a saucepan. Remove from the heat and stir in the crushed biscuits and granulated sugar. Press the biscuit mixture into the base of a 23-cm/9-inch round springform cake tin. Place in the preheated oven and bake for 10 minutes. Remove from the oven and leave to cool.

3. Increase the oven temperature to 200°C/400°F/Gas Mark 6. Use a hand-held electric mixer to beat the cheese until creamy, then gradually add the caster sugar and flour and beat until smooth. Increase the speed and beat in the vanilla extract, orange rind and lemon rind, then beat in the eggs and egg yolks one at a time. Finally, beat in the cream. The mixture should be light and fluffy – beat on a faster setting if you need to.

4. Grease the sides of the cake tin and pour in the filling. Smooth the top, transfer to the oven and bake for 15 minutes, then reduce the temperature to 110°C/225°F/Gas Mark ¼ and bake for a further 30 minutes. Turn off the oven and leave the cheesecake in it for 2 hours to cool and set. Chill in the refrigerator overnight before serving.

5. Slide a knife around the edge of the cake then unclip and remove from the tin.

serves 10

cals: 744   fat: 60.1g   sat fat: 33.3g   fibre: 0.7g   carbs: 42.9g   sugar: 32.6g   salt: 1g   protein: 9.9g

tarte tatin

prep: 30 mins, plus resting
cook: 35–50 mins

200 g/7 oz caster sugar
150 g/5½ oz unsalted butter
900 g/2 lb eating apples
350 g/12 oz ready-made puff pastry
plain flour, for dusting

top tip

It's important to use eating apples in this recipe because cooking apples wouldn't hold their shape during cooking.

1. Place a 20-cm/8-inch ovenproof frying pan over a low heat and add the sugar. Melt the sugar until it starts to caramelize, but do not let it burn. Add the butter and stir it in to make a light toffee sauce. Remove from the heat.

2. Peel and core the apples and cut them into eighths. Place the apples in the pan on top of the toffee sauce, cut side up. They should fill the pan – if there are any large gaps, add a few more apple pieces. Put the pan over a medium heat and cover. Simmer, without stirring, for about 5–10 minutes, until the apples have soaked up some of the sauce, then remove from the heat.

3. Preheat the oven to 190°C/375°F/Gas Mark 5. Roll out the pastry on a lightly floured surface into a circle that will cover the pan, with a little overhanging the sides.

4. Lay the pastry round on top of the apples and tuck the edges down inside between the fruit and the pan until it is sealed. Don't worry about making it look too neat – it will be turned over before serving.

5. Put the pan into the preheated oven and bake for 25–35 minutes, checking to make sure the pastry doesn't burn. The pastry should be puffed and golden. Remove from the oven and leave to rest for 30–60 minutes.

6. To serve, make sure the tart is still a little warm and place a plate on top of the frying pan. Carefully turn it over and lift the pan off. Serve warm.

cappuccino soufflés

prep: 30 mins, plus cooling
cook: 25 mins

unsalted butter, for greasing

150 g/5½ oz plain chocolate, broken into pieces

6 tbsp whipping cream

2 tsp instant espresso coffee granules

2 tbsp coffee-flavoured rum liqueur

3 large eggs, separated, plus 1 extra egg white

2 tbsp golden caster sugar, plus extra for sprinkling

cocoa powder, for dusting

1. Preheat the oven to 190°C/375°F/Gas Mark 5. Grease six 175-ml/6-fl oz ramekins and sprinkle with caster sugar to coat.

2. Place the chocolate in a heatproof bowl set over a saucepan of gently simmering water and stir until melted. Remove from the heat and leave to cool.

3. Place the cream in a small, heavy-based saucepan and heat gently. Stir in the coffee until it has dissolved, then the liqueur. Divide the mixture between the prepared ramekins.

4. Place the egg whites in a clean, grease-free bowl and whisk until soft peaks form, then gradually whisk in the sugar until stiff but not dry. Stir the egg yolks into the cooled melted chocolate, then stir in a little of the whisked egg whites. Gradually fold in the remaining egg whites.

5. Divide the mixture between the ramekins. Place the ramekins on a baking sheet and bake in the preheated oven for 15 minutes, or until just set. Dust with cocoa.

top tip

For well-risen soufflés, ensure the oven is preheated to the correct temperature and don't open the oven before they're done.

pumpkin pies

prep: 25 mins
cook: 18–20 mins

12 ready-made all-butter
tartlet cases

200 g/7 oz canned pumpkin purée or
unsweetened pie filling

70 g/2½ oz light muscovado sugar

1 egg, plus 1 egg yolk, lightly beaten

2 tbsp maple syrup

125 ml/4 fl oz evaporated milk

1 tsp ground cinnamon

½ tsp ground ginger

¼ tsp ground cloves

softly whipped cream and freshly
grated nutmeg, to serve (optional)

1. Preheat the oven to 190°C/375°F/Gas Mark 5. Place the tartlet cases on a large baking sheet. Put the pumpkin purée and sugar into a large bowl and beat together with a wooden spoon.

2. Add the beaten egg, maple syrup, evaporated milk and spices and, using a balloon whisk, mix until thoroughly combined. Carefully pour into the tartlet cases.

3. Bake in the preheated oven for 18–20 minutes, or until the filling is just set but still slightly wobbly in the centre. Serve warm or cold, topped with a dollop of whipped cream and sprinkled with a little grated nutmeg, if using.

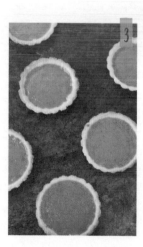

top tip

If canned pumpkin is unavailable, use steamed fresh pumpkin, mashed with a fork until smooth.

apple & blackberry crumble

prep: 25 mins
cook: 40-45 mins

900 g/2 lb cooking apples

300 g/10½ oz blackberries,
  fresh or frozen

55 g/2 oz light muscovado sugar

1 tsp ground cinnamon

custard or cream, to serve (optional)

crumble topping

85 g/3 oz white self-raising flour

85 g/3 oz wholemeal plain flour

115 g/4 oz unsalted butter, diced

55 g/2 oz demerara sugar

top tip

The crumble topping freezes successfully so it's well worth making up a double batch and freezing half for another day.

1. Preheat the oven to 200°C/400°F/Gas Mark 6. Peel and core the apples, then cut them into chunks. Put them in a bowl with the blackberries, muscovado sugar and cinnamon and mix together, then transfer to a 900-ml/1½-pint baking dish.

2. To make the crumble topping, sift the self-raising flour into a bowl and stir in the wholemeal flour. Rub in the butter with your fingertips until the mixture resembles coarse breadcrumbs. Stir in the demerara sugar.

3. Sprinkle the crumble topping evenly over the fruit and bake in the preheated oven for 40–45 minutes, or until the apples are soft and the topping is golden brown and crisp. Serve with custard or cream, if using.

serves 6

cals: 401   fat: 16.5g   sat fat: 10g   fibre: 6.7g   carbs: 63.3g   sugar: 36g   salt: 0.4g   protein: 4.5g

banoffee meringue pie

prep: 20–25 mins
cook: 12–15 mins

20-cm/8-inch ready-made all-butter round pastry case

400 g/14 oz canned dulce de leche (caramel sauce)

1 large banana

3 large egg whites

175 g/6 oz caster sugar

1 tbsp chocolate shavings

1. Preheat the oven to 190°C/375°F/Gas Mark 5. Place the pastry case on a baking sheet. Spoon the dulce de leche into the case and level the surface. Peel and thinly slice the banana and arrange the slices on top of the caramel.

2. Put the egg whites into a clean, grease-free bowl and beat with a hand-held electric mixer until they hold stiff peaks. Gradually whisk in the sugar, a spoonful at a time, to make a firm and glossy meringue. Spoon the meringue over the bananas and swirl with the back of the spoon.

3. Bake the pie in the preheated oven for 12–15 minutes, or until the meringue is golden brown. Sprinkle the chocolate shavings over the hot meringue and serve immediately or leave to cool.

variation

To make individual pies, use eight
ready-made tartlet cases and
bake for 10 minutes.

cals: 454   fat: 19.7g   sat fat: 9.5g   fibre: 2.1g   carbs: 64.3g   sugar: 48g   salt: 0.6g   protein: 5.3g

plum & almond filo tart

prep: 25-30 mins, plus cooling
cook: 24-29 mins

55 g/2 oz unsalted butter, softened

4 filo pastry sheets, each measuring 28-cm/11-inch square

1 egg

55 g/2 oz ground almonds

40 g/1½ oz caster sugar, plus 1 tbsp extra for sprinkling

1 tbsp plain flour

5 small red plums, stoned and quartered

custard, to serve (optional)

1. Preheat the oven to 200°C/400°F/Gas Mark 6. Place a baking sheet in the oven to preheat. Melt 15 g/½ oz of the butter and use some to lightly grease a 20-cm/8-inch round, loose-based tart tin. Brush the filo pastry sheets with the remaining melted butter and layer them in the prepared tin, gently scrunching the pastry around the edges.

2. Scrunch some foil into a disc and place in the pastry case. Bake in the preheated oven for 4–5 minutes, or until the pastry is just beginning to brown around the edges. Put the remaining butter into a bowl with the egg, ground almonds, sugar and flour and beat together until smooth.

3. Remove the foil and spread the almond mixture into the pastry case. Top with the plum quarters and sprinkle with sugar. Return to the oven and bake for 15–20 minutes, or until the pastry is golden brown and the filling is almost set (it will still be wobbly in the middle). Leave to cool in the tin. Serve warm or cold with custard, if using.

top tip

If cracks appear in the filo pastry when lining the tin, brush with melted butter and patch up any holes with more buttered pastry.

serves 4

cals: 448 fat: 21.2g sat fat: 8.1g fibre: 3.8g carbs: 57.2g sugar: 23.6g salt: 0.2g protein: 9.7g

baking secrets

There are few types of cooking that are more rewarding than baking. Not only can you create irresistible sweet and savoury treats for your family and friends but the actual hands-on process of baking is also immensely satisfying, not to mention surprisingly good fun. Whilst your baked goods might not have the perfectly proportioned features of the shop-bought versions, the flavour will almost certainly be far superior and you'll also know exactly what ingredients went into them.

There's nothing difficult about baking but it is a more precise form of cooking than you may be used to and requires a certain amount of patience. However, the basic skills are really easy to learn and, as long as you follow the simple rules on the opposite page, you'll soon be confidently turning out mouth-watering cakes and bakes to the delight of everyone who gets to taste them!

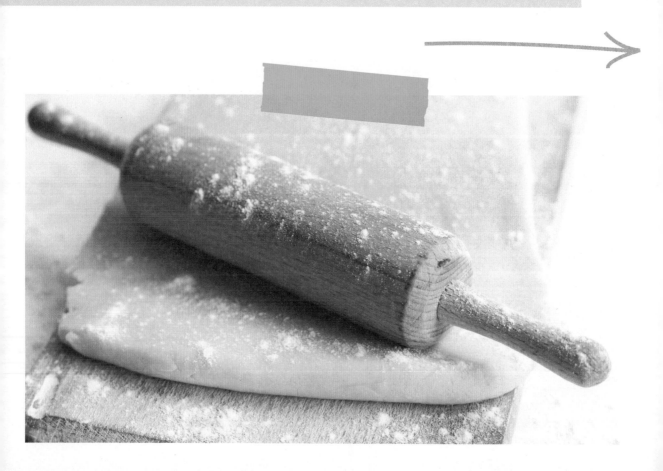

top tips

– Prepare the kitchen before you start by clearing work surfaces and making sure you have enough space to work.

– Check that you have all the ingredients you need to make the recipe – you don't want to realise that you've run out of something at a crucial moment.

– Make sure that the cake tin is the correct size and prepare it by greasing and/or lining as specified in the recipe.

– Preheat the oven to the required temperature and take eggs out of the refrigerator for at least 1 hour before starting. If the recipe requires softened butter, allow it to stand at room temperature for about 1 hour.

– For bread making, a warm kitchen will help the dough to rise so turn on the oven earlier than needed.

– For pastry making, keep hands and equipment as cool as possible to prevent the fat from melting and making the pastry sticky.

– Measure ingredients carefully and use measuring spoons for raising agents and flavourings.

– Don't be tempted to open the oven door too early – a rush of cold air can make a cake sink!

– To check if a sponge cake is ready, gently press the surface with your fingertips. It should spring back without leaving an impression. For deeper cakes or rich fruit cakes, check by inserting a skewer into the centre of the cake – it should come out clean.

– To check if bread is ready, hold the loaf with a thick tea towel and tap the base firmly with your knuckles – it should sound hollow.

– Leave cakes and bakes to cool completely before storing them in airtight tins or containers.

chocolate bread &
butter pudding

prep: 25–30 mins, plus soaking and cooling
cook: 35–40 mins

1 large brioche loaf

200 g/7 oz unsalted butter, softened, plus extra for greasing

150 g/5½ oz plain chocolate, broken into pieces

100 g/3½ oz chopped dried figs

4 large eggs

600 ml/1 pint whole milk

150 g/5½ oz caster sugar

1 tsp vanilla extract

single cream, to serve (optional)

1. Preheat the oven to 160°C/325°F/Gas Mark 3. Grease a 900-g/2-lb loaf tin and line with baking paper.

2. Slice the brioche and butter each slice on one side. Sprinkle the chocolate and figs over the buttered side of the slices. Put the slices back into the shape of the loaf and fit into the prepared tin.

3. In a medium-sized bowl whisk together the eggs, milk, sugar and vanilla extract, then pour the mixture over the brioche and allow to soak for 5 minutes.

4. Bake in the preheated oven for 35–40 minutes, or until golden and set in the middle. Leave to cool for 10 minutes before serving with cream, if using.

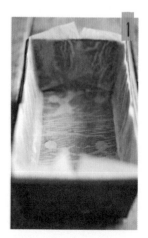

top tip

This is a handy recipe for using up slightly stale brioche or bread.

cals: 676   fat: 39.8g   sat fat: 21.1g   fibre: 3.9g   carbs: 68.6g   sugar: 41.8g   salt: 0.5g   protein: 12.8g

peach cobbler

prep: 30 mins
cook: 35 mins

6 peaches, peeled, stoned and sliced
4 tbsp caster sugar
½ tbsp lemon juice
1½ tsp cornflour
½ tsp almond extract or vanilla extract
ice cream, to serve (optional)

topping
185 g/6½ oz plain flour
115 g/4 oz caster sugar
1½ tsp baking powder
½ tsp salt
85 g/3 oz unsalted butter, diced
1 egg
5–6 tbsp milk

variation

This recipe can easily be adapted to make the most of seasonal gluts of fruit Instead of the peaches, try halved apricots or plums.

1. Preheat the oven to 220°C/425°F/Gas Mark 7. Place the peaches in a 23-cm/9-inch square baking dish. Add the sugar, lemon juice, cornflour and almond extract and toss together. Bake in the preheated oven for 20 minutes.

2. Meanwhile, to make the topping, sift the flour, all but 2 tablespoons of the sugar, the baking powder and salt into a bowl. Rub in the butter with your fingertips until the mixture resembles breadcrumbs. Beat the egg and 5 tablespoons of the milk in a jug, then mix into the dry ingredients with a fork until a soft, sticky dough forms. If the dough seems too dry, stir in the extra tablespoon of milk.

3. Reduce the oven temperature to 200°C/400°F/Gas Mark 6. Remove the peaches from the oven and drop spoonfuls of the topping over the surface, without smoothing. Sprinkle with the remaining sugar and bake for a further 15 minutes, or until the topping is golden brown and firm – the topping will spread as it cooks. Serve hot or at room temperature with ice cream, if using.

cals: 416   fat: 13.6g   sat fat: 8g   fibre: 3.1g   carbs: 69.1g   sugar: 42.8g   salt: 0.9g   protein: 6.3g

baked lemon cheesecake

prep: 25 mins, plus chilling and cooling
cook: 45-50 mins

55 g/2 oz unsalted butter, plus extra
  for greasing
175 g/6 oz gingernut biscuits, crushed
3 lemons
300 g/10½ oz ricotta cheese
200 g/7 oz Greek-style yogurt
4 eggs, beaten
1 tbsp cornflour
100 g/3½ oz caster sugar
strips of lemon zest, to decorate

1. Preheat the oven to 180°C/350°F/Gas Mark 4. Grease a 20-cm/8-inch springform cake tin and line with baking paper.

2. Melt the butter in a saucepan and stir in the crushed biscuits. Press into the base of the prepared cake tin. Chill in the refrigerator until firm.

3. Meanwhile, finely grate the rind from the lemons into a bowl and squeeze in the juice. Add the ricotta, yogurt, eggs, cornflour and caster sugar and whisk to form a smooth batter.

4. Spoon the mixture into the tin. Bake in the preheated oven for 40–45 minutes, or until just firm and golden brown.

5. Leave the cheesecake to cool completely in the tin, then run a knife around the edge to loosen and turn out onto a serving plate. Decorate with lemon zest.

top tip

This cheesecake is even more delicious served with a spoonful of crème fraîche or natural yogurt

cals: 326   fat: 16.9g   sat fat: 9.8g   fibre: 0.7g   carbs: 34g   sugar: 21.9g   salt: 0.5g   protein: 9.8g

spiced pear & sultana strudel

prep: 35 mins
cook: 25–30 mins

3 firm, ripe pears, peeled, cored
  and diced
juice and finely grated rind of ½ lemon
75 g/2¾ oz demerara sugar
1 tsp ground allspice
55 g/2 oz sultanas
55 g/2 oz ground almonds
6 sheets filo pastry
  (half a 250-g/9-oz pack)
85 g/3 oz unsalted butter, melted,
  plus extra for greasing
icing sugar, for dusting

1. Preheat the oven to 200°C/400°F/Gas
Mark 6. Grease a baking sheet.

2. Mix together the pears, lemon juice and
rind, demerara sugar, allspice, sultanas and
half the ground almonds.

3. Place two sheets of filo pastry, slightly
overlapping, on a clean tea towel. Brush lightly
with melted butter and sprinkle with a third of
the almonds. Top with two more sheets of filo,
more melted butter and half the remaining
ground almonds. Repeat once more.

4. Spread the pear mixture down one side,
to within 2.5 cm/1 inch of the edge. Roll the
pastry over to enclose the filling and roll up,
using the tea towel to lift. Transfer to the
prepared baking sheet and tuck the ends
under.

5. Brush the strudel with the remaining
melted butter and bake in the preheated oven
for 20–25 minutes, until golden and crisp.
Serve warm or cold, dusted with icing sugar.

top tip

Placing the filo pastry on a clean tea towel makes it much easier to roll it around the filling.

cals: 448   fat: 19.1g   sat fat: 8.6g   fibre: 5.3g   carbs: 66g   sugar: 29.8g   salt: 0.2g   protein: 6.7g

black-bottom pecan pie

prep: 40 mins, plus chilling and cooling
cook: 40 mins

300 g/10½ oz plain flour, plus extra
   for dusting

1 tsp salt

1 tsp sugar

225 g/8 oz chilled unsalted butter, diced,
   plus extra for greasing

6–8 tbsp iced water, plus extra
   if needed

filling

90 g/3¼ oz milk chocolate chips

2 tbsp cocoa powder

4 eggs

60 g/2¼ oz soft light brown sugar

60 g/2¼ oz granulated sugar

135 ml/4½ fl oz golden syrup

55 g/2 oz unsalted butter, melted

150 g/5½ oz pecan nut halves

1. To make the pastry, put the flour, salt and sugar into a bowl and mix to combine. Add the butter and rub in with your fingertips until the mixture resembles coarse breadcrumbs. Carefully add the water, a teaspoon at a time, until the mixture just begins to crumble. Add more water if necessary to achieve the right consistency.

2. Turn out the pastry onto a lightly floured work surface and knead until pliable. Wrap in clingfilm and chill in the refrigerator for at least 1 hour.

3. Preheat the oven to 180 °C/350 °F/Gas Mark 4. Grease a 23-cm/9-inch round tart tin. Remove the pastry from the refrigerator and leave to warm up to room temperature. Roll out the pastry on a lightly floured work surface and use to line the prepared tin.

4. To make the filling, put the chocolate chips and cocoa powder into a heatproof bowl set over a saucepan of gently simmering water and stir until melted. Spread the mixture over the base of the unbaked pastry case.

5. Put the eggs, brown sugar and granulated sugar into a bowl and beat to combine. Add the golden syrup and melted butter and mix until incorporated. Stir in the pecan nuts, then pour the filling into the pastry case.

6. Bake in the preheated oven for 30 minutes, or until the filling is just set. Leave to cool in the tin.

top tip

This classic pie (with a twist)
is particularly tasty served cold
with whipped cream.

cals: 736   fat: 48.4g   sat fat: 22.3g   fibre: 3.7g   carbs: 68.4g   sugar: 36.2g   salt: 0.9g   protein: 10.6g

blood orange polenta tart

prep: 25 mins, plus cooling
cook: 41–43 mins

cooking oil spray
250 g/9 oz cooked polenta or cornmeal
55 g/2 oz soft light brown sugar,
   plus 1 tbsp
3 blood oranges or small navel oranges

filling

4 eggs
140 g/5 oz caster sugar
150 ml/5 fl oz orange juice
1 tbsp lemon juice
125 ml/4 fl oz milk
½ tsp vanilla extract
1 tsp finely grated orange rind

fact

At just over 200 calories per serving, this zesty dessert is a great option if you're watching your weight. Serve with natural yogurt as a lighter alternative to cream.

1. Preheat the oven to 180°C/350°F/Gas Mark 4. Spray a 23-cm/9-inch springform cake tin with cooking oil spray.

2. To make the case, combine the cooked polenta with 55 g/2 oz of the brown sugar in a bowl and mix well. Spread the mixture into a thin layer in the prepared tin. Bake in the preheated oven for about 20 minutes, or until it begins to brown.

3. To make the filling, whisk together the eggs, caster sugar, orange juice, lemon juice, milk and vanilla extract. Stir in the orange rind, then pour the mixture onto the polenta case in an even layer. Return to the oven and bake for about 15 minutes, or until the filling begins to set.

4. While the tart is baking, slice the oranges into thin slices, using a serrated knife. When the filling is partly set, remove the tart from the oven and arrange the orange slices on top. Sprinkle the remaining tablespoon of brown sugar over the top and return the tart to the oven. Bake for a further 6–8 minutes, or until the filling is mostly set.

5. Remove from the oven and place the tin on a wire rack to cool.

cals: 202   fat: 3.5g   sat fat: 1.2g   fibre: 1.2g   carbs: 38.2g   sugar: 32.2g   salt: 0.3g   protein: 5g

zebra puddings

prep: 35-40 mins
cook: 20-25 mins

125 ml/4 fl oz vegetable oil, plus extra for greasing

125 g/4½ oz caster sugar

4 tbsp milk, plus extra if needed

2 eggs, beaten

150 g/5½ oz self-raising flour, sifted, plus extra for dusting

½ tsp baking powder

15 g/½ oz cocoa powder, sifted

sauce

300 ml/10 fl oz double cream

200 g/7 oz plain chocolate, chopped

1 tbsp golden syrup

25 g/1 oz unsalted butter

1. Grease six 175-ml/6-fl oz metal pudding basins or dariole moulds and dust with flour. Preheat the oven to 180°C/350°F/Gas Mark 4.

2. Place the oil, sugar, milk and eggs in a mixing bowl and gently whisk to combine. Divide the mixture between two bowls.

3. Sift 100 g/3½ oz of the flour and ¼ teaspoon of the baking powder into one of the bowls and fold to combine. Sift the remaining flour and baking powder together with the cocoa into the other bowl and mix well. Make sure that both mixtures have the same consistency; pourable but not runny. If they need to be looser, add a little more milk.

4. Pour a little of the plain mixture into each of the pudding basins to cover the base. Pour a little of the chocolate mixture into the centre of each, then repeat with the plain mixture. Repeat, alternating the mixtures until both have been used up.

5. Transfer the pudding basins to a baking sheet. Bake in the preheated oven for 20–25 minutes, until well risen and a skewer inserted into the centre comes out clean.

6. Meanwhile, make the sauce. Heat the cream in a saucepan until just below boiling point. Stir in the chocolate, golden syrup and butter, and mix gently until the chocolate has melted. The sauce should be smooth and glossy.

7. Turn the puddings out of the basins whilst still warm, then pour over the hot sauce and serve immediately.

top tip

When building the sponge mixtures, always pour into the centre to form a 'zebra' pattern.

makes 6

cals: 886   fat: 68.2g   sat fat: 27.9g   fibre: 3.6g   carbs: 61.6g   sugar: 37.3g   salt: 1g   protein: 8.1g

Cooking with yeast is not particularly difficult and the results can be most rewarding. Of course, you do need more time to produce yeasted products but for the most part they can be left alone to rise, leaving you free to do other things. Using easy-blend dried yeast, rather than fresh yeast, speeds up the process too.

bread & savouries

crusty white loaf ———————————→ 156

five-seed loaf ———————————————→ 158

sourdough bread ———————————→ 160

irish soda bread ———————————→ 162

tomato & rosemary focaccia ————→ 164

spicy jalapeño cornbread ————————→ 166

sausage rolls ———————————————→ 168

spring onion & cheese tart ————→ 170

BREAD-MAKING ———————————————→ 172

margherita pizza ————————————→ 174

crumpets ———————————————————→ 176

individual chicken pies ——————→ 178

garlic & herb bread spirals ——————→ 180

walnut & pecorino scones ————————→ 182

crispy bacon muffins ——————————→ 184

stromboli with salami & peppers ————→ 186

english muffins ————————————————→ 188

beef & stout pies ————————————→ 190

crusty white loaf

prep: 35 mins, plus rising and cooling
cook: 30 mins

1 egg
1 egg yolk
150–200 ml/5–7 fl oz lukewarm water
500 g/1 lb 2 oz strong white flour,
  plus extra for dusting
1½ tsp salt
2 tsp sugar
1 tsp easy-blend dried yeast
25 g/1 oz butter, diced
sunflower oil, for greasing

top tip

Bread freezes well so it's worth making extra when time is plentiful. Freeze for up to one month, then thaw at room temperature and refresh in a hot oven for 5 minutes.

1. Place the egg and egg yolk in a jug and beat lightly to mix. Add enough of the lukewarm water to make up to 300 ml/ 10 fl oz. Stir well.

2. Place the flour, salt, sugar and yeast in a large bowl. Add the butter and rub it in with your fingertips until the mixture resembles breadcrumbs. Make a well in the centre, add the egg mixture and work to a smooth dough.

3. Turn out the dough onto a lightly floured work surface and knead for about 10 minutes, or until smooth and elastic. Brush a bowl with oil. Shape the dough into a ball, place it in the bowl and cover with a damp tea towel. Leave to rise in a warm place for 1 hour, or until doubled in volume. Oil a 900-g/2-lb loaf tin.

4. Turn out the dough onto a lightly floured surface and knead for 1 minute, or until smooth. Shape the dough the length of the tin and three times the width. Fold the dough into three lengthways and place it in the tin with the join underneath. Cover and leave in a warm place for 30 minutes, or until it has risen above the tin. Preheat the oven to 220°C/425°F/Gas Mark 7.

5. Bake the loaf in the preheated oven for 30 minutes, or until firm and golden brown. Test that the loaf is cooked by tapping on the base with your knuckles – it should sound hollow. Transfer to a wire rack to cool.

cals: 2,292   fat: 46.5g   sat fat: 18.4g   fibre: 13.4g   carbs: 396.6g   sugar: 14.9g   salt: 9.6g   protein: 89.1g

five-seed loaf

prep: 25 mins, plus rising and cooling
cook: 25-30 mins

300 g/10½ oz strong wholemeal flour

225 g/8 oz strong white flour, plus extra for dusting

1 tsp salt

100 g/3½ oz mixed seeds (including sesame, pumpkin, sunflower, hemp and linseeds)

2 tsp easy-blend dried yeast

1 tbsp soft light brown sugar

2 tbsp sunflower oil, plus extra for greasing

300 ml/10 fl oz lukewarm water

1. Lightly grease a baking sheet with oil. Mix the wholemeal flour, white flour, salt, seeds and yeast in a large bowl. Stir in the sugar. Mix together the oil and water. Make a well in the centre of the dry ingredients and pour in the liquid. Mix with a knife to make a soft, sticky dough.

2. Turn out the dough onto a lightly floured work surface and knead for 5–7 minutes, or until smooth and elastic. Shape the dough into a ball and place on the prepared baking sheet. Dust the top of the loaf with wholemeal flour and leave in a warm place for 1–1½ hours, or until doubled in volume. Preheat the oven to 220°C/425°F/Gas Mark 7.

3. Bake the loaf in the preheated oven for 5 minutes. Reduce the oven temperature to 200°C/400°F/Gas Mark 6 and bake for a further 20–25 minutes, or until golden brown and the base sounds hollow when tapped with your knuckles. Transfer to a wire rack to cool.

variation

For rolls, shape the dough into 12 balls and bake for 10–15 minutes at 200°C/400°F/ Gas Mark 6.

cals: 2,860   fat: 95.5g   sat fat: 11.6g   fibre: 44.8g   carbs: 365.4g   sugar: 25g   salt: 6g   protein: 109.9g

sourdough bread

prep: 50 mins, plus starter, rising and cooling
cook: 30 mins

450 g/1 lb wholemeal flour

4 tsp salt

350 ml/12 fl oz lukewarm water

2 tbsp black treacle

1 tbsp vegetable oil, plus extra
   for greasing

plain flour, for dusting

starter

85 g/3 oz wholemeal flour

85 g/3 oz strong white flour

55 g/2 oz caster sugar

250 ml/9 fl oz milk

1. For the starter, put the wholemeal flour, strong white flour, sugar and milk into a non-metallic bowl and beat well with a fork. Cover with a damp tea towel and leave to stand at room temperature for 4–5 days, until the mixture is frothy and smells sour.

2. Sift the flour and half the salt into a bowl and add the water, treacle, oil and starter. Mix well with a wooden spoon until a dough begins to form, then knead with your hands until it leaves the side of the bowl. Turn out onto a lightly floured surface and knead for 10 minutes, or until smooth and elastic.

3. Brush a bowl with oil. Shape the dough into a ball, place it in the bowl and cover with a damp tea towel. Leave to rise in a warm place for 2 hours, or until doubled in volume.

4. Dust two baking sheets with flour. Mix the remaining salt with 4 tablespoons of water in a bowl. Turn out the dough onto a lightly floured work surface and knock back with your fist, then knead for a further 10 minutes. Halve the dough, shape each piece into an oval and place the loaves on the prepared baking sheets. Brush with the saltwater glaze and leave to stand in a warm place, brushing frequently with the glaze, for 30 minutes.

5. Preheat the oven to 220°C/425°F/Gas Mark 7. Brush the loaves with the remaining glaze and bake for 30 minutes, or until the crust is golden brown and the bases of the loaves sound hollow when tapped with your knuckles. If it is necessary to cook them for longer, reduce the oven temperature to 190°C/375°F/Gas Mark 5. Transfer to wire racks to cool.

makes 2 loaves

top tip

You'll need to prepare the starter for this rustic loaf a few days in advance of baking.

cals: 1,408   fat: 22.8g   sat fat: 4.7g   fibre: 29.8g   carbs: 269.1g   sugar: 44.9g   salt: 12.1g   protein: 46.5g

irish soda bread

prep: 25 mins, plus cooling
cook: 25–30 mins

butter, for greasing

450 g/1 lb plain flour, plus extra
   for dusting

1 tsp salt

1 tsp bicarbonate of soda

400 ml/14 fl oz buttermilk

1. Preheat the oven to 220 °C/425 °F/Gas Mark 7. Lightly grease a baking sheet.

2. Sift the dry ingredients into a mixing bowl. Make a well in the centre, pour in most of the buttermilk and mix well using your hands. The dough should be very soft but not too wet. If necessary, add the remaining buttermilk.

3. Turn out the dough onto a floured work surface and knead for about 10 minutes. Shape into a 20-cm/8-inch round.

4. Place on the prepared baking sheet and cut a cross in the top. Bake in the preheated oven for 25–30 minutes, or until golden brown and the base sounds hollow when tapped with your knuckles. Transfer to a wire rack to cool.

fact

This quick and easy-to-make Irish bread uses bicarbonate of soda as a raising agent instead of yeast cals: 1,970   fat: 20.7g   sat fat: 11g   fibre: 12.9g   carbs: 372.6g   sugar: 22.1g   salt: 10g   protein: 64.3g

tomato & rosemary focaccia

prep: 30 mins, plus rising and cooling
cook: 20 mins

500 g/1 lb 2 oz strong white flour, plus extra for dusting

1½ tsp salt

1½ tsp easy-blend dried yeast

2 tbsp chopped fresh rosemary, plus extra sprigs to garnish

6 tbsp extra virgin olive oil, plus extra for greasing

300 ml/10 fl oz lukewarm water

1 tsp coarse sea salt

6 oven-dried or sun-blush tomato halves, sliced in half

variation

It's so easy to ring the changes with this traditional Italian bread by using different toppings. Try adding olives, cherry tomatoes, garlic, onion, basil or even cheese.

1. Sift the flour and salt into a bowl and stir in the yeast and chopped rosemary. Make a well in the centre, pour in 4 tablespoons of the oil and mix quickly with a wooden spoon. Gradually stir in the lukewarm water but do not over-mix. Turn out onto a lightly floured work surface and knead for 2 minutes. The dough will be quite wet; do not add more flour.

2. Brush a bowl with oil. Shape the dough into a ball, put it in the bowl and cover with a damp tea towel. Leave to rise in a warm place for 2 hours, until the dough has doubled in volume.

3. Brush a baking sheet with oil. Turn out the dough onto a lightly floured surface and knock back with your fist, then knead for 1 minute. Put the dough on the prepared baking sheet and press out into an even layer. Cover the baking sheet with a damp tea towel. Leave to rise in a warm place for 1 hour.

4. Preheat the oven to 240°C/475°F/Gas Mark 9. Whisk the remaining oil with a little water in a bowl. Dip your fingers into the oil mixture and press them into the dough to make dimples all over. Sprinkle with the sea salt. Press the tomato pieces into some of the dimples, drizzle with the remaining oil mixture and sprinkle the loaf with the rosemary sprigs.

5. Bake in the preheated oven for 20 minutes, until golden brown. Transfer to a wire rack to cool slightly, then serve warm.

cals: 2,617   fat: 89.2g   sat fat: 12.7g   fibre: 15.9g   carbs: 366.5g   sugar: 9.1g   salt: 16g   protein: 81.8g

spicy jalapeño cornbread

prep: 25 mins, plus cooling
cook: 40 mins

1 tbsp vegetable oil

4 fresh jalapeño chillies, halved, deseeded and thinly sliced

1 spring onion, thinly sliced

1 tbsp chopped fresh parsley

275 g/9¾ oz polenta

185 g/6½ oz plain flour

2 tbsp sugar

1 tbsp baking powder

1 tsp salt

3 eggs

450 ml/15 fl oz single cream

100 g/3½ oz butter, melted, plus extra for greasing

1. Heat the oil in a small frying pan. Add the chillies, spring onion and parsley and sauté for 2 minutes, until softened. Remove from the heat and set aside.

2. Preheat the oven to 190°C/375°F/Gas Mark 5. Grease a 25-cm/10-inch square cake tin.

3. Mix together the polenta, flour, sugar, baking powder and salt in a large bowl. Put the eggs, cream, butter and chilli mixture into a separate large bowl and stir to combine. Add the wet ingredients to the polenta mixture and mix to a firm batter.

4. Pour the batter into the prepared tin. Bake in the preheated oven for 30 minutes, or until a skewer inserted into the centre comes out clean. Leave to cool in the tin for 5 minutes, then turn out onto a wire rack to cool completely. Cut into 12 bars.

makes 12

fact

Polenta (or cornmeal) gives this yeast-free bread a lovely golden colour and distinctive flavour.

cals: 324   fat: 17.3g   sat fat: 9.8g   fibre: 1.9g   carbs: 33.9g   sugar: 3.1g   salt: 1.1g   protein: 6.5g

sausage rolls

prep: 30 mins, plus soaking
cook: 20-25 mins

2 tsp milk, plus extra for brushing

20 g/¾ oz white bread, crusts removed, diced

400g/14 oz sausage meat

1 onion, finely chopped

1 egg

1 egg yolk

½ tbsp ground cumin

1 tsp paprika

450 g/1 lb ready-made puff pastry

plain flour, for dusting

beaten egg white, for brushing

salt and pepper

1. Preheat the oven to 180°C/350°F/Gas Mark 4. Line a large baking sheet with baking paper.

2. Put the milk into a large bowl, add the bread and leave to soak until soft. Add the sausage meat, onion, egg, egg yolk, cumin and paprika. Season to taste with salt and pepper, then mix well.

3. Roll out the pastry on a lightly floured work surface and cut out 12 x 13-cm/5-inch squares. Brush the pastry squares with the egg white. Spread the sausage meat mixture evenly down the centre of each square, then roll up the pastry to enclose the filling.

4. Transfer to the prepared baking sheet, seam-side down, and brush with milk. Bake in the preheated oven for 20–25 minutes, until golden and cooked through.

top tip

Most supermarkets sell sausage meat in large tubes. If unavailable, just buy pork sausages and squeeze the meat out of the casings.

makes 12

cals: 286   fat: 19.7g   sat fat: 8.3g   fibre: 1.3g   carbs: 19.7g   sugar: 1.4g   salt: 1.4g   protein: 7.2g

spring onion & cheese tart

prep: 25–30 mins, plus resting and cooling
cook: 50 mins

1 tbsp vegetable oil, plus extra
   for oiling
3–4 spring onions, finely chopped
3 eggs
150 g/5½ oz Emmenthal cheese, grated
150 g/5½ oz cooked ham, diced
200 ml/7 fl oz double cream
pinch of freshly grated nutmeg
salt and pepper

pastry
200 g/7 oz plain flour
pinch of salt
125 g/4½ oz butter, at room
   temperature
125 ml/4 fl oz water

1. To make the pastry, mix together the flour, salt and butter in a bowl. Add the water, a little at a time, mixing after each addition until a stiff dough forms. Wrap in clingfilm and leave to rest for 1 hour.

2. Preheat the oven to 180 °C/350 °F/Gas Mark 4. Oil a 25-cm/10-inch rectangular fluted flan dish. Heat the oil in a frying pan over a medium heat, add the spring onions and fry for about 5 minutes, until translucent. Remove from the heat and leave to cool.

3. Beat the eggs in a large bowl, then add the cheese and ham and mix to combine. Add the cream and spring onions and mix well. Stir in the nutmeg, then season to taste with salt and pepper.

4. Press the pastry into the prepared dish and prick the base all over with a fork. Pour the filling into the pastry case and bake in the bottom of the preheated oven for 45 minutes, until the surface of the tart is golden brown and a skewer inserted into the centre comes out clean. Serve hot or cold.

cals: 463   fat: 35.4g   sat fat: 20.5g   fibre: 0.9g   carbs: 20.4g   sugar: 0.8g   salt: 1.5g   protein: 15.8g

bread-making

There are so many different kinds of home-made breads that they could easily fill a book by themselves. Making bread is a useful skill and can be a rewarding and satisfying pastime.

Yeast is the raising agent most frequently used for breads. It is a living organism that, when active, creates carbon dioxide. Small bubbles of carbon dioxide become trapped within the structure of the dough, giving bread its characteristic texture.

There are two main types of yeast available: fresh and dried.

Fresh yeast

This can be purchased from bakeries and health food stores. It has a creamy colour and is moist and firm. Fresh yeast is usually dissolved in liquid and left for a preliminary fermentation before being added to the remaining ingredients. It will only keep for a few days in the refrigerator, but can be frozen for up to three months.

Dried yeast

This is available in two forms. Regular dried yeast requires a preliminary fermentation and is activated by mixing it with a little liquid and sugar or flour. Easy-blend dried yeast, fast-action yeast and instant dried yeast are all different names for yeast that does not require this preliminary fermentation and is simply stirred

into the flour before the liquid is added. Dried yeast has a much longer shelf life than fresh yeast and does not need to be refrigerated.

Yeast works quickest in warm temperatures, so it is generally recommended that the dough is left in a warm place to rise. However, yeast does not stop working at low temperatures – it simply slows down. Therefore, dough can be made, shaped and left to rise overnight in a refrigerator. Allow the dough to return to room temperature

before baking. Many bakers believe that yeast that is left to work in slower conditions produces a loaf with more flavour and character.

Unlike pastry, there is no need for exercising caution when working with bread dough – a firm hand is perfect for kneading and developing the gluten content. Gluten is formed by a combination of two proteins, gliadin and glutenin, which are found in wheat flour. Strong bread flours have a higher proportion of these than regular flour. When the proteins are hydrated, they bond with each other, creating a large protein called gluten that gives the bread its structure. The longer the dough is kneaded, the stronger the gluten becomes and the better texture the bread has. It is possible to knead the dough so much that it becomes too warm and the gluten begins to break down, but this is unlikely to happen if

kneading by hand. If kneading in a mixer, process in short bursts, stopping for a few seconds in between.

Yeast-free breads

Some breads do not contain yeast. These breads use another method to leaven them (make them rise) or are unleavened. Sometimes called 'quick breads', soda bread and corn bread fall into the first category – bicarbonate of soda or baking powder is used as a raising agent. Carbon dioxide is produced as soon as the dough is mixed, so the bread must be baked immediately. Unleavened breads are sometimes called 'flat breads'. Some flat breads, such as naan and pitta bread, are in fact leavened with yeast or baking powder but unleavened dough can also be used. Paratha, tortillas and chapattis are all examples of yeast-free flat breads.

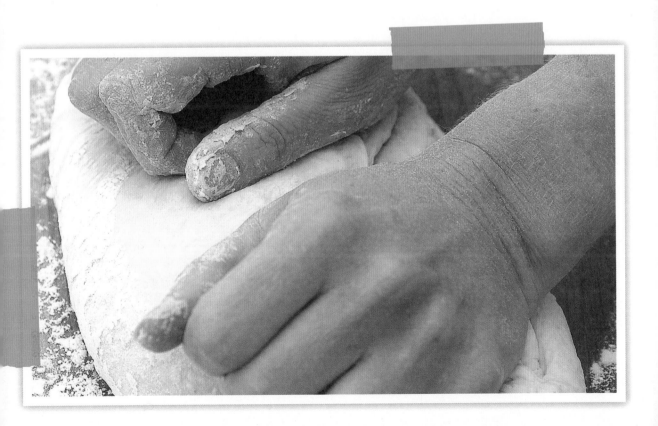

margherita pizza

prep: 35-40 mins, plus rising
cook: 40-50 mins

15 g/½ oz butter

1 tbsp olive oil, plus extra for brushing and drizzling

1 small onion, finely chopped

200 g/7 oz canned chopped tomatoes

1 tbsp tomato purée

brown sugar, to taste

1 tbsp chopped fresh basil, plus extra leaves for the topping

3 tbsp water

140 g/5 oz mozzarella cheese, sliced

4 tomatoes, sliced

2 tbsp grated Parmesan cheese

salt and pepper

pizza dough

225 g/8 oz strong white flour, plus extra for dusting

1 tsp salt

½ tsp easy-blend dried yeast

1 tbsp olive oil

150 ml/5 fl oz lukewarm water

1. To make the pizza dough, sift the flour and salt into a bowl and stir in the yeast. Make a well in the centre and pour in the oil and lukewarm water, then mix to a soft dough. Turn out onto a lightly floured surface and knead for 10 minutes, until smooth and elastic. Put into an oiled bowl, cover and leave to rise in a warm place for about 1 hour, until doubled in volume.

2. Melt the butter with the oil in a saucepan. Add the onion and cook over a low heat, stirring occasionally, for 5 minutes, until softened. Stir in the canned tomatoes, tomato purée, sugar, chopped basil and water. Season to taste with salt and pepper. Increase the heat to medium and bring to the boil, then reduce the heat and simmer, stirring occasionally, for 15–20 minutes, until thickened.

3. Preheat the oven to 220°C/425°F/Gas Mark 7. Brush a baking sheet with oil. Knock back the dough and knead briefly on a lightly floured surface. Roll out into a round and transfer to the prepared baking sheet. Push up a rim all the way around.

4. Spread the tomato sauce evenly over the pizza base. Arrange the mozzarella and tomato slices on top. Coarsely tear the basil leaves and put them on the pizza, then sprinkle with the Parmesan. Drizzle with oil and bake in the preheated oven for 15–20 minutes, until crisp and golden.

crumpets

prep: 25 mins, plus resting
cook: 12-15 mins

230 g/8¼ oz strong white flour
1 tsp baking powder
½ tsp salt
230 ml/8¼ fl oz lukewarm milk
150 ml/5 fl oz lukewarm water
1 tsp easy-blend dried yeast
oil, for greasing and frying

1. Sift together the flour, baking powder and salt into a large bowl. Gradually add the milk and water, adding the yeast halfway through. Whisk vigorously until the mixture is the consistency of double cream.

2. Cover the bowl with clingfilm and leave to rest for 1 hour at room temperature, until the mixture has expanded and bubbles have formed in it.

3. Oil four individual 8-cm/3¼-inch crumpet rings and heat some oil in a large, heavy-based frying pan. Place the rings in the pan and pour 2–3 tablespoons of mixture into each ring. Gently fry until the tops are dry or have developed small holes.

4. Remove the crumpet rings using a palette knife. Turn over the crumpets and cook for 1–2 minutes, until cooked through. Repeat until all the mixture has been used, oiling the rings and pan when necessary.

top tip

Crumpets are best eaten hot from the pan. Butter or jam are typical toppings, but other accompaniments include cheese or fried eggs.

makes 10

cals: 123   fat: 3.8g   sat fat: 0.8g   fibre: 0.7g   carbs: 17.3g   sugar: 1.3g   salt: 0.5g   protein: 4.4g

individual chicken pies

prep: 30 mins, plus standing
cook: 1 hour 5 mins-1¼ hours

1 tbsp olive oil

225 g/8 oz button mushrooms, sliced

1 onion, finely chopped

350 g/12 oz carrots, sliced

2 celery sticks, sliced

1 litre/1¾ pints cold chicken stock

85 g/3 oz butter

55 g/2 oz plain flour, plus extra
   for dusting

900 g/2 lb skinless, boneless chicken
   breasts, cut into 2.5-cm/1-inch cubes

115 g/4 oz frozen peas

1 tsp chopped fresh thyme

675 g/1 lb 8 oz ready-made
   shortcrust pastry

1 egg, lightly beaten

salt and pepper

1. Preheat the oven to 200°C/400°F/Gas Mark 6. Heat the oil in a large saucepan. Add the mushrooms and onion and cook over a medium heat, stirring frequently, for 8 minutes, until golden.

2. Add the carrots, celery and half the stock and bring to the boil. Reduce the heat to low and simmer for 12–15 minutes, until the vegetables are almost tender.

3. Meanwhile, melt the butter in a large saucepan over a medium heat. Whisk in the flour and cook, stirring constantly, for 4 minutes.

4. Gradually whisk in the remaining stock, then reduce the heat to low–medium and simmer, stirring, until thick. Stir in the vegetable mixture and add the chicken, peas and thyme.

5. Simmer, stirring constantly, for 5 minutes. Taste and adjust the seasoning, adding salt and pepper if needed. Divide the mixture between six large ramekins.

6. Roll out the pastry on a floured work surface and cut out six rounds, each 2.5 cm/1 inch larger than the diameter of the ramekins.

7. Place the pastry rounds on top of the filling, then crimp the edges. Cut a small cross in the centre of each round.

8. Put the ramekins on a baking sheet and brush the tops with beaten egg. Bake in the preheated oven for 35–40 minutes, until golden brown and bubbling. Leave to stand for 15 minutes before serving.

top tip

You can also use leftover roast chicken to make these comfort food classics.

makes 6

cals: 925   fat: 52.7g   sat fat: 21.6g   fibre: 6.6g   carbs: 65.3g   sugar: 7.1g   salt: 4.1g   protein: 46.3g

garlic & herb bread spirals

prep: 40 mins, plus rising and cooling
cook: 25-30 mins

500 g/1 lb 2 oz strong white flour,
  plus extra for dusting
2¼ tsp easy-blend dried yeast
1½ tsp salt
350 ml/12 fl oz lukewarm water
2 tbsp olive oil, plus extra for greasing
85 g/3 oz butter, melted and cooled
3 garlic cloves, crushed
2 tbsp chopped fresh parsley
2 tbsp snipped fresh chives
beaten egg, for glazing
sea salt, for sprinkling

variation

These tear-and-share bread swirls make a tasty alternative to garlic baguette. For variety, add different herbs to the butter or spread with pesto instead.

1. Brush a large baking sheet with oil. Combine the flour, yeast and salt in a mixing bowl. Stir in the water and half the oil, mixing to a soft, sticky dough.

2. Turn out the dough onto a lightly floured work surface and knead until smooth and no longer sticky. Return to the bowl, cover with a damp tea towel and leave to rise in a warm place for about 1 hour, until doubled in volume.

3. Preheat the oven to 240°C/475°F/Gas Mark 9. Mix together the butter, garlic, herbs and the remaining oil. Roll out the dough to a 33 x 23-cm/13 x 9-inch rectangle and spread the herb mix evenly over the dough to within 1 cm/½ inch of the edge.

4. Roll up the dough from one long side and place on a board, seam-side down. Cut into 12 thick slices and arrange, cut-side down, on the prepared baking sheet, spaced about 2 cm/¾ inch apart.

5. Cover and leave to rise in a warm place until doubled in size and springy to the touch. Brush with beaten egg and sprinkle with sea salt. Bake in the preheated oven for 20–25 minutes, until golden brown and firm. Transfer to a wire rack to cool.

cals: 237   fat: 9.4g   sat fat: 4.2g   fibre: 1.3g   carbs: 30.4g   sugar: 0.4g   salt: 1.4g   protein: 7.2g

walnut & pecorino scones

prep: 20-25 mins, plus cooling
cook: 15 mins

450 g/1 lb self-raising flour,
  plus extra for dusting

pinch of salt

85 g/3 oz butter, diced,
  plus extra for greasing

50 g/1¾ oz caster sugar

50 g/1¾ oz pecorino cheese, grated

100 g/3½ oz walnut pieces

about 300 ml/10 fl oz milk

butter, to serve (optional)

1. Preheat the oven to 200°C/400°F/Gas Mark 6. Grease a baking sheet.

2. Sift the flour and salt into a large bowl. Add the butter and rub it in with your fingertips until the mixture resembles fine breadcrumbs. Stir in the sugar, cheese and walnuts. Stir in enough of the milk to bring the mixture together into a soft dough.

3. Gently roll the dough out on a lightly floured work surface until it is about 2.5–3 cm/1–1¼ inches thick. Cut out 16 circles with a 6-cm/2½-inch plain round cutter. Place on the prepared baking sheet.

4. Bake in the preheated oven for 15 minutes, or until golden brown and firm to the touch. Transfer to a wire rack to cool. Serve spread with butter, if using.

top tip

Savoury scones are scrumptious eaten warm with salted butter and a mature, tangy cheese. They also make a great accompaniment to soup.

makes 16

cals: 221   fat: 10.8g   sat fat: 4.4g   fibre: 1.2g   carbs: 26.2g   sugar: 4.3g   salt: 1.3g   protein: 5.2g

crispy bacon muffins

prep: 25-30 mins, plus cooling
cook: 28 mins

oil or melted butter, for greasing
  (if using)
250 g/9 oz rindless, smoked streaky
  bacon
7 tbsp sunflower oil
1 onion, finely chopped
280 g/10 oz plain flour
1 tbsp baking powder
2 eggs
250 ml/9 fl oz buttermilk
salt and pepper

top tip

Bacon may sound like an unusual filling for a muffin but, trust us, it works! Serve these mouth-watering morsels for breakfast or pack into a lunchbox with a flask of soup.

1. Preheat the oven to 200°C/400°F/Gas Mark 6. Grease a 12-hole muffin tin or line with 12 paper cases.

2. Chop the bacon, reserving three rashers to garnish. Cut each of the reserved rashers into four pieces and set aside.

3. Heat 1 tablespoon of the oil in a frying pan. Add the onion and cook for 2 minutes. Add the chopped bacon and cook for about 5 minutes, stirring occasionally, until crispy. Remove from the heat and leave to cool.

4. Sift together the flour and baking powder into a large bowl.

5. Lightly beat the eggs in a large jug or bowl, then beat in the buttermilk and the remaining oil. Make a well in the centre of the dry ingredients, pour in the beaten liquid ingredients and add the bacon mixture. Season to taste with salt and pepper. Stir gently until just combined; do not over-mix.

6. Spoon the mixture into the prepared muffin tin. Place one of the reserved pieces of bacon on top of each muffin.

7. Bake in the preheated oven for about 20 minutes, until well risen, golden brown and firm to the touch. Leave to cool in the tin for 5 minutes, then serve warm.

cals: 259   fat: 14.5g   sat fat: 3.3g   fibre: 0.9g   carbs: 20.3g   sugar: 1.7g   salt: 1.5g   protein: 11.3g

stromboli with salami & peppers

prep: 40-45 mins, plus rising and standing
cook: 30-35 mins

500 g/1 lb 2 oz strong white flour, sifted, plus extra for dusting

2¼ tsp easy-blend dried yeast

2 tsp sea salt

3 tbsp olive oil, plus extra for greasing and brushing

350 ml/12 fl oz lukewarm water

filling

85 g/3 oz thinly sliced Italian salami

175 g/6 oz mozzarella cheese, chopped

25 g/1 oz basil leaves

2 red peppers, roasted, peeled, deseeded and sliced (or ready-roasted peppers from a jar)

pepper

top tip

Stromboli is an Italian-American invention that is rather like a rolled-up pizza. Its portable shape means that it is great to take along to a picnic.

1. Mix together the flour, yeast and 1½ teaspoons of the sea salt, then stir in the oil with enough of the water to make a soft dough.

2. Knead the dough on a lightly floured work surface for about 10 minutes, until smooth and elastic. Cover and leave to rise in a warm place for 1 hour, or until doubled in volume.

3. Lightly knead for 2–3 minutes, until smooth. Cover and leave for a further 10 minutes.

4. Roll out the dough to a 38 x 25-cm/ 15 x 10-inch rectangle with a thickness of 1 cm/½ inch.

5. Preheat the oven to 200°C/400°F/Gas Mark 6. Arrange the salami over the dough and top with the mozzarella cheese, basil and red peppers. Season to taste with pepper.

6. Oil a baking sheet. Firmly roll up the dough from a long side, pinch the ends and place on the prepared baking sheet, seam-side down. Cover and leave to stand for 10 minutes.

7. Pierce the roll deeply with a skewer several times. Brush with oil and sprinkle with the remaining sea salt. Bake in the preheated oven for 30–35 minutes, or until firm and golden. Serve warm.

makes 1 loaf

cals: 3,304   fat: 128.9g   sat fat: 42g   fibre: 20.9g   carbs: 382.2g   sugar: 17g   salt: 17.9g   protein: 146.2g

english muffins

prep: 30-40 mins, plus rising
cook: 30-35 mins

450 g/1 lb strong white bread flour,
  plus extra for dusting

½ tsp salt

1 tsp caster sugar

1½ tsp easy-blend dried yeast

250 ml/9 fl oz lukewarm water

125 ml/4 fl oz natural yogurt

vegetable oil, for brushing

40 g/1½ oz semolina

top tip

If not eating the muffins straightaway, leave them to cool completely at the end of step 5, then store in an airtight container for up to 48 hours.

1. Sift the flour and salt together into a bowl and stir in the sugar and yeast. Make a well in the centre and add the lukewarm water and yogurt. Stir with a wooden spoon until the dough begins to come together, then knead with your hands until it comes away from the sides of the bowl.

2. Turn out onto a lightly floured work surface and knead for 5–10 minutes, until smooth and elastic. Brush a bowl with oil. Shape the dough into a ball, place it in the bowl and cover with a damp tea towel. Leave to rise in a warm place for 30–40 minutes, until the dough has doubled in volume.

3. Dust a baking sheet with flour. Turn out the dough onto a lightly floured work surface and knead lightly. Roll out to a thickness of

2 cm/¾ inch. Stamp out 12 circles with a 7.5-cm/3-inch plain round cutter and sprinkle each round with semolina.

4. Transfer the muffins to the prepared baking sheet, cover with a damp tea towel and leave to rise in a warm place for 30–40 minutes.

5. Heat a griddle or large frying pan over a medium–high heat and brush lightly with oil. Add half the muffins and cook for 7–8 minutes on each side, until golden brown. Cook the remaining muffins in the same way.

6. To serve, split the muffins in half and toast lightly.

cals: 165   fat: 1.5g   sat fat: 0.4g   fibre: 1.2g   carbs: 30.4g   sugar: 1.2g   salt: 0.3g   protein: 6.8g

beef & stout pies

prep: 40 mins, plus cooling
cook: 2 hours 20 mins–2 hours 25 mins

3 tbsp plain flour

900 g/2 lb braising beef, cut into 2.5-cm/1-inch pieces

4–5 tbsp vegetable oil

300 ml/10 fl oz meat stock

1 onion, roughly chopped

225 g/8 oz chestnut mushrooms, stalks discarded, caps quartered

1 tbsp tomato purée

2 tsp chopped fresh thyme

250 ml/9 fl oz stout

450 g/1 lb ready-made puff pastry

1 egg yolk, lightly beaten

salt and pepper

1. Combine the flour with 1 teaspoon of salt and ½ teaspoon of pepper in a bowl, then toss the beef in the mixture until evenly coated.

2. Heat 3 tablespoons of the oil in a large frying pan over a medium–high heat. Brown the beef, in batches, and transfer to a flameproof casserole. Deglaze the frying pan with 4 tablespoons of the stock, and add the liquid to the casserole.

3. Heat the remaining oil in the frying pan and cook the onion and mushrooms for 6–7 minutes, until soft. Add to the casserole with the tomato purée, thyme, stout and the remaining stock. Place the casserole over a medium–high heat and bring to the boil, then simmer gently, with the lid slightly askew, for 1½ hours. Check the seasoning, adding salt and pepper if needed.

4. Drain the meat mixture in a sieve set over a bowl, reserving the liquid. Leave until cool. Preheat the oven to 220°C/425°F/Gas Mark 7. Put a baking sheet in the oven to preheat.

5. Divide the meat mixture between four 400-ml/14-fl oz pie dishes. Pour in enough of the liquid to not quite cover the filling. Dampen the rims of the pie dishes.

6. Divide the pastry into quarters. Roll out each piece to about 2.5 cm/1 inch bigger than the dish. Cut a 1-cm/½-inch strip from each piece of pastry and press it onto a dampened rim. Brush with egg yolk, then drape the rolled-out pastry on top, covering the strip. Trim and crimp the edges and make three slashes down the middle.

7. Decorate the tops of the pies with pastry shapes cut from the trimmings. Brush with the remaining egg yolk.

8. Place on the preheated baking sheet and bake for 20 minutes. Reduce the oven temperature to 200°C/400°F/Gas Mark 6 and bake for a further 5 minutes, until golden.

top tip

For best results and a not-so-humble pie, use a good-quality stout or dark ale.

makes 4

cals: 1,070   fat: 54.5g   sat fat: 19.4g   fibre: 3.8g   carbs: 56.4g   sugar: 5.7g   salt: 3.4g   protein: 82.1g

index

almonds
  cranberry & ginger florentines 102
  frosted carrot cake 16
  pistachio & almond tuiles 92
  plum & almond filo tart 136
  polenta & blueberry loaf cake 32
  raspberry & almond cake 36
  rich fruit cake 14
  soured cream cake with
    nectarines 38
  spiced pear & sultana strudel 146
apples
  apple & blackberry crumble 132
  apple pie 120
  apple streusel cupcakes 48
  caramelized apple tarts 110
  dorset apple cake 20
  tarte tatin 126

bacon muffins, crispy 184
bananas: banoffee meringue pie 134
basic techniques 64–65
beef & stout pies 190–191
berries
  apple & blackberry crumble 132
  cranberry & ginger florentines 102
  summer fruit tartlets 82
  see also blueberries; raspberries;
    strawberries
blondies 56
blueberries
  blueberry cheesecake bars 74
  blueberry tarts 104–105
  polenta & blueberry loaf cake 32
bread-making 172–173
breads
  crusty white loaf 156
  english muffins 188
  five-seed loaf 158
  garlic & herb bread spirals 180
  irish soda bread 162
  sourdough bread 160
  spicy jalapeño cornbread 166
  tomato & rosemary focaccia 164

cake pops 72
cake tins, lining 26–27
cakes
  chocolate macaroon gateau 116
  classic chocolate cake 8
  coconut layer cake 24
  coffee bundt cake 18–19
  cookie ice-cream cake 40–41
  dorset apple cake 20
  frosted carrot cake 16
  hot chocolate fudge layer cake 30
  lemon drizzle cake 10
  piñata party cake 42–43
  polenta & blueberry loaf cake 32
  pumpkin spice cake 34
  raspberry & almond cake 36
  red velvet cake 28
  rich fruit cake 14
  soured cream cake with
    nectarines 38

victoria sponge cake 12
  see also cheesecake; cupcakes;
    macaroons; muffins; whoopie pies
carrot cake, frosted 16
cheese
  margherita pizza 174
  spring onion & cheese tart 170
  walnut & pecorino scones 182
  see also cream cheese
cheesecake
  baked lemon cheesecake 144
  blueberry cheesecake bars 74
  new york cheesecake 124
cherries
  morello cherry clafoutis 96
  rich fruit cake 14
chicken pies, individual 178–179
chocolate 65, 101
  black-bottom pecan pie 148
  blondies 56
  cake pops 72
  cappuccino soufflés 128
  chocolate bread & butter
    pudding 140
  chocolate caramel squares 60
  chocolate chip cookies 46
  chocolate macaroon gateau 116
  chocolate pretzel fudge squares 68
  classic chocolate cake 8
  cookie ice-cream cake 40–41
  cranberry & ginger florentines 102
  hot chocolate fudge layer cake 30
  mocha puddings 122
  pain au chocolat cinnamon
    rolls 106
  profiteroles 108
  red velvet cake 28
  rocky road chocolate muffins 50
  white chocolate passion éclairs
    112–113
  white chocolate-dipped
    madeleines 88
  zebra puddings 152–153
cinnamon scones 114
coconut
  coconut layer cake 24
  cranberry & ginger florentines 102
coffee
  cappuccino soufflés 128
  coffee bundt cake 18–19
  mocha puddings 122
cookies
  chocolate chip cookies 46
  cookie ice-cream cake 40–41
  jam rings 54
  red velvet crinkle cookies 62
cream cheese
  baked lemon cheesecake 144
  blueberry cheesecake bars 74
  coconut layer cake 24
  fluffy gingerbread cupcakes 76–77
  frosted carrot cake 16
  new york cheesecake 124
  pumpkin spice cake 34
  red velvet cake 28

soured cream cake with
  nectarines 38
summer fruit tartlets 82
croissants 86
crumpets 176
cupcakes
  apple streusel cupcakes 48
  fluffy gingerbread cupcakes 76–77
  summer garden cupcakes 58–59

dates
  rich fruit cake 14
  sticky toffee pudding 22
doughnuts, powdered 94

essential ingredients 100–101

flapjacks, raisin 78
florentines, cranberry & ginger 102

garlic & herb bread spirals 180

jam rings 54

lemons
  baked lemon cheesecake 144
  lemon drizzle cake 10
  luscious lemon whoopie pies 52
  new york cheesecake 124
  tarte au citron 98–99

macaroons
  chocolate macaroon gateau 116
  vanilla macaroons 84
margherita pizza 174
mocha puddings 122
muffins
  crispy bacon muffins 184
  english muffins 188
  raspberry crumble muffins 70
  rocky road chocolate muffins 50

nectarines: soured cream cake with
  nectarines 38
nuts 101
  black-bottom pecan pie 148
  see also almonds; walnuts

oranges
  blood orange polenta tart 150
  new york cheesecake 124

passion fruit: white chocolate passion
  éclairs 112–113
pastries
  croissants 86
  pain au chocolat cinnamon rolls 106
  profiteroles 108
  raspberry & rosewater éclairs 90–91
  sausage rolls 168
  white chocolate passion éclairs
    112–113
  see also pies & tarts
peach cobbler 142
pear & sultana strudel, spiced 146

pies & tarts
  apple pie 120
  banoffee meringue pie 134
  beef & stout pies 190–191
  black-bottom pecan pie 148
  blood orange polenta tart 150
  blueberry tarts 104–105
  caramelized apple tarts 110
  individual chicken pies 178–179
  plum & almond filo tart 136
  pumpkin pies 130
  spring onion & cheese tart 170
  summer fruit tartlets 82
  tarte au citron 98–99
  tarte tatin 126
piñata party cake 42–43
pistachio & almond tuiles 92
plum & almond filo tart 136
polenta
  blood orange polenta tart 150
  polenta & blueberry loaf cake 32
  spicy jalapeño cornbread 166
profiteroles 108
pumpkin
  pumpkin pies 130
  pumpkin spice cake 34

raisins & sultanas
  cinnamon scones 114
  frosted carrot cake 16
  raisin flapjacks 78
  rich fruit cake 14
  spiced pear & sultana strudel 146
  sticky toffee pudding 22
raspberries
  raspberry & almond cake 36
  raspberry & rosewater éclairs 90–91
  raspberry crumble muffins 70
red velvet cake 28
red velvet crinkle cookies 62
rocky road chocolate muffins 50

sausage rolls 168
scones
  cinnamon scones 114
  walnut & pecorino scones 182
sourdough bread 160
sticky toffee pudding 22
strawberries
  strawberry & cream whoopie pies 66
  victoria sponge cake 12
stromboli with salami & peppers 186

tomato & rosemary focaccia 164
top tips 138–139
tuiles, pistachio & almond 92

victoria sponge cake 12

walnuts
  pumpkin spice cake 34
  walnut & pecorino scones 182
whoopie pies
  luscious lemon whoopie pies 52
  strawberry & cream whoopie pies 66